Guido
Italian/American Youth and Identity Politics

Edited by

Letizia Airos & Ottorino Cappelli

Bordighera Press

Library of Congress Control Number: 2011914098

COVER ART: *"Senza titolo" by Darrell Fusaro*

A heart-felt thanks to Giulia Prestia
for her keen editorial sensitivity and acute translation capability.

Printed in the United States.

Published by
BORDIGHERA PRESS
John D. Calandra Italian American Institute
25 West 43rd Street, 17th Floor
New York, NY 10036

VIA FOLIOS 69
ISBN 978-1-59954-026-9

VIA FOLIOS 69

Table of Contents

It Takes a Forum (9)
Preface by Letizia Airos

The Name of the Guido. An Exercise in Italian/American Identity Politics **(13)**
Introduction by Ottorino Cappelli

1. Discussions

Real Italians (39)
by Joseph Sciorra

Dialogue and Debate: Not Denigration and Dismissal (44)
by Fred Gardaphé

Guidos and Negros (50)
by Jerry Krase

The Situation (55)
by Robert Viscusi

Stereotype, Caricature, or Lifestyle? (63)
by Chiara and Franco Montalto

On Guidos, Gramsci, and Irony Deficiency (67)
by Laura E. Ruberto

Organized Culture (69)
by Fred Gardaphé

2. Interviews

Italian Americans in the Trap of Television (75)
Interview with Maria Laurino

Guido: A Generational Rebellion (79)
Interview with Donna M. Chirico

Italian Americans between Guidos and Columbus (83)
Interview with Nancy Carnevale

Dirty Laundry and Deep Rugs (86)
Interview with Gianfranco Norelli

The View from Italy (89)
Interview with Aldo Grasso

3. The Colloquium

Guido: An Italian/American Youth Style (101)
by Anthony Julian Tamburri

Guidos on MTV: Tangled Up in the Feedback Loop (106)
by Donald Tricarico

Keyword: Different. What Guidos Are, and Are Not (115)
by Johnny DeCarlo

Thoughts from a Former Guidette—Turned Senator (118)
by Diane Savino

4. Contributors

Editors and Contributors (125)

Guido
Italian/American Youth and Identity Politics

It Takes a Forum
by Letizia Airos

This time the Internet truly shuffled the deck. Thanks to i-Italy. org, the guido subculture, a phenomenon that is both challenged and appropriated by the Italian/American community, was discussed openly, generated political debate and intellectual controversy, and became well-known even in Italy.

Without the Internet, and without our multimedia portal dedicated to Italian/American issues, there only would have been the usual ping-pong between American television stations and major Italian/American organizations about the guido phenomenon and the television program *Jersey Shore* on MTV. A handful of seconds to express its outrage through mainstream media outlets—that's all that the Italian/American community would have achieved.

Instead, a discussion that first began in academia grew larger with i-Italy's involvement—publicizing and broadcasting the symposium Guidos: An Italian American Lifestyle organized by the John D. Calandra Italian American Institute—which then crossed over to the 'Net, presenting a collective analysis of the phenomenon to its very foundation. These were not fruitless protests covered for a few seconds by the media of the "dominant culture," but lengthy, articulate, clear analyses that were open to all.

This is because the nature of the Internet, fortunately, makes any attempt at control hard, to say the least. The Internet is like a collective mind, someone has said, but one that does not think in a one-sided manner: it opens up to the world in its complexity and it also reveals—perhaps above all—the contradictions. Today we can no longer think of analyzing any socio-political phenomenon without referring to this collective mind, rendered increasingly more global with the advent of social networks.

Marshall McLuhan once declared: the medium is the message. It creates a pervasive effect on the collective imagination regardless of the content of the information conveyed from time to time. It was 1968, and the fascination/fear of technology as an extension of our senses attracted/repelled many observers. But, and though it seems strange to say, there were only radio and television at the time.

Communication then, for the first time, narrowed space and time, and united the world into one big "global village." But the age of interactivity had not yet arrived. Many feared—and perhaps with good reason—the capacity of this one-way medium, television, to control and guide people in one single direction. And no one dreamed that people could speak, or that the viewers could interact with each other.

This perspective has changed dramatically with the Internet, a medium that really does recreate the global village, that is, a global network of human interaction. It also facilitates a certain type of content with respect to others, especially those who are not acceptable to mainstream channels. Practically everyone has noticed, from students on American college campuses to young Egyptians who recently took to the streets of Cairo with the communicative and organizational strength granted to them by Facebook, Twitter, and other social networks.

We have seen this growing awareness in our "small Italian/American world," in the editorial staff of i-Italy that I coordinate. There has never been an Italian/American place where everyone—literally—could participate and share their opinions. Circulate it, read it, make it count.

The voices have steadily grown to a large number. Worlds little known to the general public have come to light, whether they are Italian, American, or Italian/American. And, for example, some have discovered for the first time that not all Italian Americans agree with an attitude of mere censorship—especially when a movie or a reality show deals with issues that are considered "offensive to the Italian American identity" (such as *Jersey Shore* today or *The Sopranos* several years ago). And they agree even less when censorship is expected to extend to research activities, attempting to prevent a group of intellectuals from organizing a symposium at the Calandra Institute precisely on the sociological phenomenon of the guido lifestyle.

In this way even the self-proclaimed leaders and activists of the Italian/American community have had to deal with the open and pluralistic reality of the Internet, and they have even come together in our space. This created a wonderful dialogue, difficult at times, but a dialogue nevertheless.

And besides this, there also developed a dialogue among readers who previously did not have a voice. Most importantly, it brought to the table an Italian/American world that had not had many opportunities to address a wider audience. The Internet, in short, performed a miracle: it allowed intellectuals to leave their ivory towers to speak to the Italian/American community and a larger audience, even in Italy, demonstrating their ability to tackle and examine social phenomena that are undesirable or even "disturbing."

The contributions collected in this book, in fact, were first published on i-Italy.org; they were read, critiqued, and have, in turn, created a hornet's nest in terms of readers' reactions. The writers shared their own views on the phenomenon that, at that time, was filling newspapers and television programs. The community's "dirty laundry" was finally aired in public, without maintaining the convention of *bella figura* (making a good impression), as a modern and pluralistic community does and should do.

i-Italy has done so by acting as a forum, a place for public discussion as well as a media sounding board to debate the themes of Italian/American identity, culture, and lifestyle. It is significant that not only did the *New York Times* join in with a long article on the symposium organized by the Calandra Institute, but also that *Corriere della Sera*—the most widespread and authoritative Italian newspaper— covered it through its media critic Aldo Grasso, who also appeared on i-Italy, giving a thoughtful and incisive interview that compares various aspects of Italy and Italian America.

So the 'Net and a new online magazine are present at the time of fracture, re-discussion, and reconsideration of an identity that also involves youth culture. It takes a forum. Until now this was lacking within the Italian/American community. We created it and we are proud.

The Name of the Guido
A Case Study in Italian/American Identity Politics
by Ottorino Cappelli

> *The old man was silent. He held both hands open on the book, as if caressing its pages, flattening them the better to read them, or as if he wanted to protect the book from a raptor's talons.*
>
> *"All of this, in any case, has been to no avail," William said to him. "Now it is over. I have found you, I have found the book, and the others died in vain."*
>
> *"Not in vain," Jorge said. "Perhaps there were too many of them. And if you needed proof that this book is accursed, you have had it. And to ensure they have not died in vain, one more death will not be too many."*
>
> *He spoke, and with his fleshless, diaphanous hands he began slowly tearing to strips and shreds the limp pages of the manuscript, stuffing them in his mouth, slowly swallowing as if he were consuming the host and he wanted to make it flesh of his flesh.*

Umberto Eco, The Name of the Rose·

In fall 2009, MTV launched what would become a highly successful if controversial reality show called *Jersey Shore* that portrayed the daily and nightly life of a group of young Italian Americans of questionable appearance and demeanor who defined themselves as guidos and guidettes. Even before the show appeared on American television, the leaders of some Italian/American[1] organizations launched an all-out anti-defamation campaign demanding that it be cancelled. *Jersey Shore*, protesters said, contained deeply offensive anti-Italian stereotypes—beginning with the very term guido: origi-

---

· Umberto Eco, *The Name of the Rose* (New York, Harvest Books, 1994) 480.

[1] I follow here Anthony Tamburri's suggestion to use a slash in place of the more common hyphen for the couplet Italian/American in its adjectival form. According to Tamburri, the hyphen has a sign-function of separateness and disjunction, creating a physical as well as an ideological gap between the terms Italian and American. The slash, on the contrary, helps bridge that double gap by establishing an egalitarian and dialectical relationship between the two terms. Only the slash and what it signifies, I would submit, allows us to speak of an Italian/American "ethnic nation" in the sense used in this essay. See Anthony Julian Tamburri, *To Hyphenate or Not to Hyphenate: The Italian/American Writer: An Other American* (Montreal, Guernica Editions, 1991).

nally a derogatory term for working-class, urban Italian Americans, which since the 1970s and 1980s has come to refer to heavily gelled, overly-muscled, poorly educated Italian youngsters with an overtly macho attitude and their female cohorts.

While Italian/American activists closed ranks in their quest for "politically correct censorship," in January 2010 the Calandra Institute of Queens College, City University of New York—the largest U.S. university research institute dedicated to the Italian/American experience—announced a colloquium entitled Guido: An Italian-American Youth Style. It was intended to analyze not the MTV show, but the social phenomenon it claimed to represent. Invited to discuss the matter were Professor Donald Tricarico, a sociologist at Queensborough Community College, CUNY who has devoted much of his academic career to the study of Italian/American youth subcultures, and Johnny DeCarlo, a young restaurateur from New Jersey, prolific blogger, and self-professed guido.

The announcement of the colloquium, sent to the Calandra Institute's mailing list, stated its background and objectives:

> The debut of MTV's reality show *Jersey Shore* and the subsequent anti-defamation charges by national ethnic organizations such as the NIAF, the OSIA, and UNICO National illustrate how little is understood about this contemporary form of Italian-American youth culture. As Prof. Tricarico has observed, "Italian-American intellectual and political elites cannot pretend that Guido is a figment of the media imaginary" (VIA 2007, 82-83).
>
> [...] Professor Donald Tricarico [has] looked at New York City's "Guido" subculture of the 1980s as a dynamic, adaptive expression of nontraditional ethnicity [...]. [He] has also written about Guido as an expression of identity politics in the northeast and about the culture's online manifestations.
>
> The main purpose of this colloquium is, indeed, to inform the public at large of this "other" facet of Italian Americana.

As soon as the message hit the inboxes of thousands of addressees, a number of exponents of the Italian/American community vehemently objected to the Calandra Institute's initiative, demanding that the colloquium be cancelled or even calling for a boycott should it take place.

In a series of blogs and private emails—whose authors shall remain anonymous to protect their privacy—the protesters stated, first of all, that they felt "besmirched" by the suggestion that they understood little about Italian/American youth culture. Indeed, one wrote demonstrating exactly the opposite: "Certainly no Italian American young man wants to be known as Guido, no young woman wants to be called a Guidette, just as no black person wants to be known as a Nigger." Still others, apparently ignorant of the distinction between scientific study and propaganda, were appalled that the Calandra Institute "would even attempt to study and then *add credence* to the idea that Italian Americans or some of them are in fact Guidos or Guidettes."

This idea that by engaging in academic research on any given topic scholars would "make it seem good," was particularly widespread among the protesters. One of them was "incensed" that the Calandra Institute was "spewing such vituperation" by presenting a "disturbing topic" as some "academically-explained" subculture; this was nothing but "ethnic self-loathing," and was tantamount to supporting, validating, and even "glorifying" both the guido phenomenon and its representation by MTV. "There is no intellectual explanation for the acceptance of the 'guido' expression" and it should not be suggested to "young and impressionable minds" that anything as a "guido subculture" exists in Italian America and should be "accepted." "What program is next," asked another without appreciating the intrinsic irony of his question, "a deep understanding of Mafia pop culture?"

For some of those antagonists who had even less control over their terminology, the "so-called intellectuals" of the Calandra Institute had been "trapped by their own Bull Shit," while Professor Tricarico was "the poster *idiot* who glorifies guido" and who, "regardless of his ancestry, does not deserve to be called an Italian American."

"Why has his name come out of the sewer where it belongs," the same blogger asked, and why has the Calandra Institute invited him "to promote his love for the term guido and all that it stands for?" The missive continued:

> Why in the world would anyone let alone Calandra invite this guy to spread his whacky destructive views about Italian Americans. In its own way it would be like a Jewish Institute inviting a Holocaust denier not only to speak but promote him for his "dynamic expression of ethnicity."
>
> [People like Tricarico] provide cover. They give "legitimacy" to shows like Jersey Shore and more to the point give those who put on this crap their justification right from an Italian American *professor* and his "famous" essay glorifying the life style of the Italian guido.
>
> [...] There is no value giving credibility by debating someone who will glorify a term like guido, or ginny or wop. Or the lifestyle it reflects. The best he deserves is pity. Guido, wop, ginny the only place those terms and the stereotypes they reflect deserve to be is buried deep in a garbage pail never to be seen again. The very same fate I wish for *Jersey Shore*.

It should be noted that reference to what the Jewish community would have been able to achieve in a similar situation also reflected a common, perhaps subliminal anti-Semitic feeling. For instance, one asked: "Could you picture the outrage, if a show like *Jersey Shore* depicted Jews as money hungry individuals and blamed them for the economic disaster we are now going through?" The answer was censorship and self-censorship. Indeed, "[t]hat type of show won't even make it to the cutting room. And you would not see Jewish intellectuals trying to 'understand that culture.'"

The political message was clear. It was a call for the total, monolithic unity of the Italian/American "nation" against the enemy—both the enemy from outside (anti-Italian media) and the enemy from within (guidos themselves and those so-called intellectuals who glorified them). Indeed, for the protesters the main effect of the Calandra Institute's announced colloquium would be "a severe blow to the extremely galvanizing effect that *Jersey Shore* has had in awakening many Italian Americans to this battle." As another put it: "The fact that we cannot even get together as one voice fighting this terminology explains why Italian Americans are the most discriminated group in New York."

The bottom line was this: Not only should the MTV show not be aired, but the Calandra Institute colloquium should not take place as well. "I suggest that you reconsider the content of this and *do the right thing*," read an email sent to the Institute's staff. Another asked more explicitly to "reconsider going forward with this lecture." And still another plainly stated "my message is boycott this guy [Professor Tricarico]."

Despite the opposition, the colloquium was held as planned on the morning of Thursday, January 21, 2010, and it was a success that went beyond the organizers' expectations. The Calandra Institute's 60-seat conference room was packed, and many other attendees followed the proceedings from a screening in the gallery, an ample space normally reserved for art exhibitions. In addition, approximately 100 people watched the colloquium live via the Institute's web cast. Along with Professor Tricarico, Mr. DeCarlo, and the Institute's staff, representatives from Italy's Consulate General were also present, as well as New York State Senator and President of the Conference of Italian American Legislators Diane Savino who, incidentally, confessed to having been a guidette in the 1980s. (Her remarks are included in this volume.) The *New York Times* even devoted a front page, top of the fold article to the colloquium in The Arts section—attention not many Italian/American events receive.[2]

One entity that contributed greatly to publicize the event was i-Italy, an independent bilingual online magazine about "everything Italian in America."[3] Since it is directed by a group of journalists

<hr>

[2] Patricia Cohen, "Discussing That Word That Prompts Either a Fist Pump or a Scowl. 'Guido,' an Italian-American Word That Arouses Pride or Anger," The *New York Times*, January 22, 2010.
[3] While the Calandra Institute has no formal influence on i-Italy, the magazine's head-quarters are hosted at the Calandra Institute and some of its staff members contribute as

and scholars, both Italian and American, i-Italy saw as its duty to inform the public at large about what was happening. For over a month before the colloquium, i-Italy made room for all those who wished to argue against halting an intellectual investigation on the grounds of political opportunity. The intention was not to defend MTV's *Jersey Shore*, of course, nor to glorify guidos, but to assert the value of trying to better understand a specific segment of Italian/American youth subculture. i-Italy also invited its readers to reflect on why Italian/American organizations seemed to think of their role in merely "reactionary" terms—demanding censorship, sweeping disturbing topics under the rug, and repressing cultural voices and internal dissent.

This little volume collects all the materials that were published by i-Italy, including the proceedings of the colloquium itself. A few videos of the event are also available on i-Italy's TV channel at www.i-italy.org/node/13161.

In what follows, I shall propose a more general interpretation of the behavior and discursive style of the Italian/American ethno-political elites (or to use an Italian-Americanism—the *prominenti*) as it emerged on that occasion.[4]

---

writers.

[4] Terms such as "elite" and "official" when referred to Italian Americans are problematic for a number of reasons. There is no Italian/American "official" board of leaders, to begin with. What exists, instead, is a series of wealthy individuals, for the most part, who have basically declared themselves the "leaders." Historically, in the U.S., these people are known as the *prominenti* or "the prominent ones"—a term that, used "as a noun rather than an adjective...is an Italian-Americanism," according to renowned historian Philip V. Cannistraro. The term began gaining wide circulation in the mid-1920s and Cannistraro quotes the radical journalist Carlo Tresca's 1931 definition of *prominenti* as "the nouveau riche *cafoni*" of the Italian/American community. (See Philip V. Cannistraro, "The Duce and the Prominenti: Fascism and the Crisis of Italian of Italian American Leadership." *Altreitalie* 31 [July-December, 2005]). The irony of all this is that members of the academic community are not, of course, part of this self-appointed circle of leaders. Perhaps this is indeed the problem—that these different communities do not speak to each other.

The Censorship Mentality of the Prominenti

Italian/American "official" reactions to MTV's *Jersey Shore* were not unique. They were reminiscent of the many protests that the professionals of "anti-defamation politics" had staged over the years against the film and media industry for the Mafia-centered representation of Italian Americans—from *The Godfather* to *Shark Tales* to *The Sopranos.*[5] More recently, a similar campaign was launched against a videogame named Mafia II.[6] In all of these past (and basically unsuccessful) efforts we see the invocation of the censor's hand, and an avid desire to sit in the cutting room with some ethnic-political scissors at hand.

As unpleasant as this may seem to many, it is nevertheless understandable. To the extent that a melting pot never really materialized in America, ethnic prejudices do exist and anti-Italianism is part of the picture, although this is rarely recognized.[7] When Italian/American organizations react to what they see as ethnic slurs in the media, they do what they are meant to do—just like other racial and ethnic watchdog groups. Furthermore, the everlasting identification of organized crime as an Italian/American thing may well be disturbing and even damaging to the community's social reputation.

Our case, however, is different for two crucial reasons. First, *Jersey Shore* is not based on a mob stereotype: the men and women of that reality show are suburban, middle-class youths whose lifestyle may well be ill-mannered, ridiculous, and sometimes reprehensible, but not criminal. The worst that can be said is that they make people laugh at Italian Americans. But lack of irony is the supreme Italian/

---

[5] To my knowledge, the best account of Italian/American anti-defamation politics as regards the Mafia stereotype is in George DeStefano, *An Offer We Can't Refuse: The Mafia in the Mind of America* (New York, Faber & Faber, 2006).

[6] Ottorino Cappelli, "Games, Media, and Politics. Does *Mafia II* Defame Italian Americans? Interview with Andrè DiMino, i-Italy, August 28, 2010 (http://www.i-italy.org/node/15313).

[7] See William J. Connell, Fred Gardaphé, eds., *Anti-Italianism: Essays on a Prejudice* (New York, Palgrave Macmillan, 2010).

American deficiency, as Fred Gardaphé pointed out in his contribution to the discussion.[8] And, once even laughter is censored, there might be no limits to what is deemed offensive and therefore not permissible. As Umberto Eco reminds us in *The Name of the Rose*, laughter was seen as the worst heresy by medieval censors.

Second, this time the anti-defamationists were not asking to just shut down an allegedly offensive TV show; they were also denying the very existence of the *social phenomenon* that was being represented (rightly or wrongly is a different matter) in the show. And, more importantly, they attempted to prevent a public discussion of that phenomenon, insulting scholars and attacking a university institute for promoting its intellectual investigation. By equating the study of a social phenomenon with its legitimation or even "glorification," and by demanding that scholarly research be stopped on the grounds that it would lend ammunition to the enemy, they blurred the lines between culture and propaganda and tried to put (ethnic) "politics" in command not only of the media but of cultural production itself. To take Eco's analogy further, Italian/American anti-defamationists were not just censoring laughter, but a *book* on laughter. Just like the medieval monk Jorge, rather than allow anyone else to read Aristotle's book on laughter, the *prominenti* chose censorship and tried to eat its pages.

As noted by some contributors to this volume, such attitudes may be interpreted as the consequence of a nationalistic-totalitarian mentality. As writer Maria Laurino says in her interview, similar phenomena can be seen all over the world. "It's the result of a sort of fervent...ethnic nationalism [that] is only about pride and doesn't allow for any kind of questioning or dissent." She points as an example to the case of Ohran Pamuk, the Turkish Noble Prize for Literature who was brought to court for having "offended the Turkish identity" by revealing to the foreign press how dangerous it is in Turkey even today to talk about the genocide of Armenians under

---

[8] See below, page 44.

20

the Ottoman Empire. "Of course we don't have trials against dissidents here in the U.S.," says Laurino, "but I think the root of the problem is the same: the notion that national pride, or in this case ethnic pride, should never be challenged."[9]

Although the generalization is suggestive and well-founded, an even deeper understanding of this matter can be gained by focusing on the specific cultural heritage of Italian/American "ethnic nationalism." This is brought to light in the conversation between Aldo Grasso and Letizia Airos when the well-known Italian media analyst states: "As for Italian Americans, I think they carry the rhetoric of Fascism with them. Historically there hasn't been a way for them to absorb and process the change. They understood the stereotype of one national identity, but they have not gone through the process of understanding the next one."[10]

Both Laurino's ethno-nationalist explanation and Grasso's suggestion that its Italian/American version has distinct Italian roots in Fascist rhetoric deserve to be investigated further.

Nationalism and Ethno-Nationalism

Let's first define the notion of "nationalism" as it is used here—or indeed "ethno-nationalism," which may be more correct.[11]

Nationalism, for our purposes, is a distinctive type of "identity politics" that typically emerges during a people's fight for the independence of their fatherland against a foreign or colonial power. At its foundation lay a sentiment of unity rooted in basic shared characteristics such as a common land, language, and cultural traditions. During the fight for independence, nationalist political elites

---

[9] See below, page 78.

[10] See below, page 96.

[11] The literature on nationalism and ethno-nationalism is so ample, of course, that it could hardly be squeezed into a footnote. Most of the subjects discussed here—and in particular, how an immigrant minority may come to adopt a nationalist agenda, and how liberal or totalitarian its rhetoric (if not its politics) may be—can be found in the excellent collection edited by Ronald Beiner, *Theorizing Nationalism* (New York, SUNY Press, 1999).

embed such sentiment into a public discourse which serves as a tool to mobilize the people as "one single nation" while providing legitimacy to their own leadership and power.

Nationalism's hyphenated child—ethno-nationalism—shares much of the same characteristics with the parent notion, except that it may also apply to diasporic communities that have no borders to defend and whose relation to a distant fatherland may be symbolic rather than actual. Here ethno-national identity politics is grounded in the conflictual relationship a group may have with other ethnicities and/or the dominant culture of the host nation. However, the public discourse articulated by nationalist and ethno-nationalist elites is very similar, and serves similar purposes of community mobilization and political legitimation. At its core it includes:

- A forceful "us vs. them" rhetoric where "us" is the national community surrounded by enemies ("them") who oppress, hate, defame "us."
- A call for the unity of the entire community behind one single leadership capable of speaking with One Voice—the Voice of the People. This implies a profound disdain for anything that may "artificially" divide the body politic, including parties and political pluralism, disdainfully labeled "factionalism."
- A call for the intellectuals and the media to serve the national cause and be organically connected to the needs of the community as expressed by its leadership. They are expected to promote a self-aggrandizing, self-glorifying image of the national community, concealing unpleasant realities rather than critically analyzing them.

Such public discourse and the monistic ideology that underlies it are based, for all intents and purposes, on *war rhetoric*. It's no wonder that most national-liberation or anti-colonial movements have adopted some version of it during the initial stage of their existence, which often involves armed struggle.

The question is: What happens next? According to historical experience, two paths are possible once this initial stage ends. One is a democratic path: As the new nation consolidates, the nationalist movement that led to independence opens up and leaves room for a plurality of forces that struggle for power by seeking representation of social, economic, and political cleavages. Pluralism and competition become accepted norms of social interaction; a civil society emerges whose diverse "identities" are reflected by a variety of independent media; and previously "organic" intellectuals choose their side or (at the very least) their subject of critical inquiry as well as their angle of vision. In this new socio-political context the monistic warrior mentality that underlies the nationalist public discourse is replaced by a common sense of peaceful patriotism. The nation now speaks through several voices, and a healthy process of elite circulation takes place, with the old *nationalist* leaders being replaced by new *national* leaders—eventually through regular competitive elections.

But an opposite path is also possible, one that may be defined as totalitarian. Once in power, nationalist leaders may refuse to give it up and resort to a self-perpetuating strategy centered on the rhetoric of national unity. The nationalist political discourse becomes official ideology as the ruling elites argue that the nation is still in danger, surrounded and penetrated by enemies—both external and internal. The nationalist movement becomes a "party of power" and works to prevent pluralism and to silence dissent. Intellectuals and the media are reduced to cogs in a propaganda machine and forced to serve as "national education" agents. Disturbing topics are expelled from discussion, controversial books are forbidden or even burned, and censorship dominates as the populace is educated to the virtues of its true and superior identity. In other words, an autocratic, tendentially totalitarian ruling elite manufactures a "nation building" phase of political development whose duration cannot (and should not) be determined so that the power of the ruling elite itself may last indefinitely.

Obviously I am suggesting that Italian/American ethno-nationalist elites have been following the nationalist-totalitarian path. The analogy is intriguing, although one important caveat is in order. In the case of classical nationalism, the point when the nationalist mobilization phase may (or should) end can be determined with some reasonable clarity—the coming to power of new indigenous elites capable of defending the nation's borders and defeating internal counter-revolutionary forces. In other words, once the transition to an independent sovereign nation-state is achieved, a country may embark on the democratic-pluralist or the totalitarian-monistic path.

By contrast, when the notion of ethno-nationalism is applied to a diasporic community the end point of the mobilizational phase cannot be determined with the same clarity. When is an "immigrant nation" *safe*—that is, it no longer needs to fear the dominant culture, competing ethnicities, and internal divisions? When could its ethno-nationalist elites—who fought heroically to establish an ethnic conscience for their group—safely declare the war to be over? When should ethnic nation-builders dismiss their fierce nationalist rhetoric and willingly accept pluralism, deal peacefully with inter-ethnic competition, and even actively promote intra-ethnic differentiation? Is total assimilation into the host society's mainstream the ultimate goal of the ethno-nationalist struggle? Or is total hegemony over both the dominant culture and the other ethnicities the final solution? But, while the latter may well be unattainable, the former may indeed not be desirable. And, in any case, an "excess of success" may ultimately dilute ethnic identity and undermine group conscience thus making the old ethno-nationalist elites irrelevant.[12]

---

[12] Note the analogy with Robert Dahl's classic theory of the "three stages of political assimilation" of ethnic communities in America. In his seminal 1961 study of New Haven, the famed Yale political scientist found that, "[a]s the struggle for respect and acceptance [of an ethnic group] is gradually won and professional and middle-class strata emerge, the old bonds of unity must give way to disunities." In this situation, for many people ethnic politics now becomes "embarrassing or meaningless" and the political effectiveness of a purely ethnic appeal becomes negligible. According to Dahl, Italians in New Haven had reached this third stage by 1950. (See Robert A. Dahl, *Who Governs? Democracy and Power in an American City* [New Haven, Yale University Press, 2005] 59, 35-36). Such a prospect, however, must sound as a frightening threat for the *prominenti*, who then resort to ethno-nationalist rhetoric in the attempt to reverse the clock and revive the old bonds of unity—as well as their undisputed power in the community.

Paradoxically, maintaining the status quo is the best choice for ethno-nationalist elites. To the extent that the melting pot does not materialize, the fight may never be over; and the *prominenti* have a vested interest in it never being over. As long as the Nation is in danger, in fact, the rhetoric of monolithic unity will remain the crucial feature of the only accepted political discourse, and the *prominenti* can keep their position as community leaders, soldiers, and policemen—those who decide what is politically correct, permissible, representable—and scholarly analyzable. So, in a sense, the totalitarian path may become a natural temptation for ethnic-nationalist elites whose *raison d'être* is in their leading a never-ending fight against the dominant culture, other groups, and internal dissent.

If this may be a general phenomenon, in the case of Italian/Americans there are some specific factors that explain the totalitarian tendency of their elites. These can be traced back to the history of Italy itself, and to the influence of Fascism on Italy's troubled experience with nation-building, at home and abroad.

Fascism and the Rhetoric of Nation Building

Although Italy has been a unified, independent nation-sate since 1861, it only became a modern nation in the first half of the 20th century thanks to Fascism—the first mass-based movement that made nationalism the core of its public discourse.

Indeed, the first wave of Italian nationalism in the 20th century—the so-called *Risorgimento*—was mainly an elite phenomenon detached from the popular masses and thus largely ineffective as a nation-building tool.[13] For decades since Italy's unification, a predominantly rural population continued to know very little about the new masters who had defeated their kings and now ruled them. The northern elites from Piedmont despised the Southerners, whose land they

---

[13] See Manlio Graziano, *The Failure of Italian Nationhood: The Geopolitics of a Troubled Identity* (London, Palgrave Macmillan, 2010).

had conquered, as "barbarians" and as "worse than Africans."[14] The hostility was reciprocal, as indicated by the decade-long armed resistance of the brigands, whose defeat took nothing less than "a ferocious dictatorship," as Antonio Gramsci famously stated.[15] The first wave of mass expulsion of millions of emigrants, which started after the unification and lasted at least half a century, only confirmed the weakness of the new nation. Besides, for a long time neither language nor religion could work as effective unifying national forces. The new Italians—mostly poor and illiterate—continued to speak different languages, now euphemistically called dialects. And although Roman Catholicism was the dominant religion, the Church stayed at war with the new State for several decades after the Italian army had entered Rome in 1870 forcing the Pope to surrender his temporal power. In sum, before Fascism, the Italian state was a nation only geographically. After half a century of failed nation-building, the famous quote from statesman Massimo D'Azeglio in the 1860s—"Italy has been made, but Italians remain to be made"—still held true.[16]

Remaking Italy by finally making Italians was the explicit intent of Fascism. But of course *nationalizing* and *fascistizing* were one and the same thing in Mussolini's totalitarian mind. The anthem of the National Fascist Party, "Giovinezza" ["Youth"] stated:

> *Within the borders of Italy/Italians were made/*
> *Mussolini remade them/for the war of tomorrow.*[17]

---

[14] General Luigi Carlo Farini, the king's first lieutenant in Naples, wrote in a letter to Prime Minister Cavour on October 27, 1860: "What country is this? Barbarians [...]. This is not Italy, this is Africa! Compared to these *cafoni*, the Bedouins are an example of civic virtue." See Claudia Petraccone, "Nord e sud: le due civiltà," *Studi storici* 35.1-2 [1994]: 512.

[15] Antonio Gramsci: *L'Ordine nuovo 1919-1920*, edited by Valentino Gerratana and Antonio A. Santucci, (Turin, Einaudi, 1987) 422.

[16] "[P]ur troppo s'è fatta l'Italia, ma non si fanno gli Italiani." Massimo Taparelli D'Azegio, *I miei ricordi* (Turin, Einaudi, 1971) 5. (http://www.letteraturaitaliana.net/pdf/Volume_8/t207.pdf).

[17] "*Dell'Italia nei confini/furon fatti gli italiani/li ha rifatti Mussolini/per la guerra di domani.*" The complete text is reported in R. J. B. Bosworth, *Mussolini's Italy: Life Under the Fascist*

The song is an excellent summation of Fascist rhetoric. It promised a renaissance of the Italians as a people of heroes, warriors, and pioneers guided by the faith in their "immortal *patria*," and enlightened by "the vision of [Dante] Alighieri." All classes ("artisans, gentlemen, and peasants") would be "proud of being Italian" and "swear allegiance to Mussolini"—although, interestingly enough, the "poor" received a special mention.[18] But, most importantly, the one group that led the list of social categories making up the new Italian body politic were the intellectuals (the *poets*, says the song in a typical neoclassical mood). And, not surprisingly at this point, all the "renegades of the *patria*" would be "placed beneath the yoke."

Italian Fascism is a paradigmatic example of nationalist-totalitarian public discourse: the Nation would be a harmonious community, an organic body politic—healthy, masculine, and unflagging—whose head, the Duce, would articulate the One and True Voice of the People. To this end, not only elective institutions and party pluralism were devastated, but an articulated system of censorship and propaganda was set up. Censorship and propaganda were the two faces of the same totalitarian coin: the former intended to prevent undesirable content from showing up in the press, literature, radio, cinema, theater, and music; the latter meant to project through the same means the only desirable content: the *grandeur* of the new Fascist Nation, beloved within Italy and respected abroad.[19] In such a system, critical appraisal of reality or even a scholarly analysis of a disturbing social phenomenon would become politicized and censored as an anti-Italian, anti-National, and anti-Fascist crime.

It was this totalitarian version of nationalism that was success-

---

Dictatorship, 1915-1945, (London, Penguin Books, 2005) 198.

[18] "*Non v'è povero quartiere/che non mandi le sue schiere/che non spieghi le bandiere/ del fascismo redentor.*" [There is no poor neighborhood/which does not send its formations/which does not spread the flag/of Fascism, our redemption.]

[19] See Guido Bonsaver, *Censorship and Literature in Fascist Italy* (Toronto, University of Toronto Press, 2007).

fully projected onto the millions of emigrants who had left Italy (mostly from the south) between the 1880s and the 1920s and went to North America. Italy's *emigrant nation* was made of people who were not yet "Italian" when they left; they became Italian abroad, solidifying that identity during the two decades of Italian Fascism.[20] The rhetoric of Fascism helped to shape their cultural experience and their discursive style as it gave them ammunition to contrast the hostility and scorn from both the dominant culture and other immigrant groups.

Fascism and the Rhetoric of Ethno-Nation Building Abroad

Italian America's historian Philip Cannistraro brilliantly counters Giuseppe Prezzolini's and Gaetano Salvemini's opinions of who Italian emigrants were, how, and to what extent they became Italian *and* American. For Prezzolini, writing in 1931 as the head of the Casa Italiana at Columbia University, they "are not Italians, since they have never been Italians. [...] They left Italy before becoming Italian." Salvemini, the famed exiled socialist who lectured at Harvard University and eventually became a U.S. citizen, echoed in 1940: "They had never felt themselves to be Italians as long as they had been living in the old country, among people who spoke their same dialect, who had their same habits, and who were laboring under their same poverty." But whereas Prezzolini underlined—somehow snobbishly—that emigrants never became either fully Italian or truly American ("They have assumed certain American habits but at bottom they remain southern peasants, without culture, schooling, and language"), Salvemini understood that in the process of becoming American, some Italian "national consciousness awoke in them when they came in touch (which often meant blows) with groups of different national origins."[21]

---

[20] See Mark I. Choate, *Emigrant Nation: The Making of Italy Abroad* (Cambridge, Mass., Harvard University Press, 2008).

[21] Cannistraro, "The Duce and the Prominenti," op. cit., p. 77.

This process was boosted during Mussolini's two decade rule and Fascism's contribution to it was indeed crucial for several reasons. First, the regime's restrictions on emigration sent a sympathetic message to those who had left in the previous decades. Indeed, by the end of the 1920s emigration had been made more difficult—in the case of the United States, this was facilitated by the Immigration Act of 1924, which severely limited the influx of "undesirable" immigrants from southern Europe and Italy in particular.[22] By reverting to previous governments' policies of "expelling" excess labor force through emigration, Fascism was telling Italians abroad: You should not have been forced to emigrate in the first place.

At the same time, as part of its policy of making Italy a respected nation abroad, the regime also set its goal "to preserve and establish the sense of being Italian among the nation's global diaspora and, while engaged in that process, pursued the task of forging new Fascist men and women in emigrant communities."[23] The *Fasci all'Estero* were incorporated into the dictatorship's bureaucracy and, with funding from Rome and the cooperation of the consular network, worked hard both to *nationalize* and *fascistize* the emigrant communities. A far-reaching propaganda war was launched to "defend *italianità* past and present," glorify everything Italian, and project an image of Italy as a proud nation, reaching its peak in 1936 with the celebration of the newly attained Italian empire.

The long-time effect of all this on the Italian/American mind should not be underestimated. Fascism's nationalist rhetoric must have been a godsend for millions of Italians who, although "white on arrival," were relegated to a position far down the scale of ethnic virtue by widespread anti-Italian prejudice.[24] For the first time, the

---

[22] In the ten years following 1900, about 200,000 Italians immigrated annually. With the imposition of the 1924 quota, 4,000 per year were allowed.

[23] Bosworth, *Mussolini's Italy*, op. cit., p. 390.

[24] Thomas A. Guglielmo, *White on Arrival: Italians, Race, Color, and Power in Chicago, 1890-1945*, Oxford, Oxford University Press, 2004; Jennifer Guglielmo and Salvatore Salerno, eds., *Are Italians White?: How Race is Made in America* (New York: Routledge, 2003).

country that once expelled them, was offering them the motivation and the means to feel part of one proud nation, at home and abroad. As Philip Cannistraro states:

> [The] process of building ethnic identity and forging ethnic solidarity was made possible by the Fascist seizure of power in Italy: the perception of Mussolini's "achievements" at home, his popularity among Americans, and his stature as an international figure in the 1920s, all combined to allow Italian Americans for the first time to claim their national identity with pride.[25]

Thus it was through a parallel process of nation building at home and ethnic-nation building abroad that Fascism's totalitarian rhetoric became the foundation of Italian Americans' identity politics and ethno-nationalist discourse.

This is not to say that all efforts to fascistize Italians abroad were successful, and actually the relationship between Italian Americans and Fascism is not the point here. Indeed, with World War II the vast majority of Italian Americans chose their side and became "American patriots"—and previously pro-Fascist *prominenti* did contribute to this outcome.

But the sudden contrast between the recently discovered sense of ethno-national identity and the abrupt drive towards Americanization imposed a high toll on the Italian emigrant nation. Two consequences regarded the sphere of communication: Italian Americans gave up their language, as parents stopped teaching Italian to their children, largely in response to the American government's campaign "not to speak the enemy's language;" and with language they lost much of their embryonic discursive power, which had just begun to take shape in the previous two decades, couched in the now unacceptable rhetoric of Fascist nationalism.[26] Two other consequences regard-

---

[25] Cannistraro, "The Duce and the Prominenti," op. cit., p. 78.
[26] On the relationship between language and discursive power as the two missing links of the Italian/American experience see the seminal work by Robert Viscusi, "Breaking the Silence. Strategic Imperatives for Italian American Culture," *VIA* 1.1 (1990): 1-14.

ed the sphere of identity politics. Forgetting Fascism meant burying *italianità* into the private and semi-private sphere of family dinners, gala parties, and neighborhood street fairs; it also meant the severing of any meaningful political relationships with the fatherland, as anti-Fascist Italy and post-Fascist Italian America begun to develop two different, non-communicating "national" identities.

Italy and Italian America: Two "Nations" Apart?

Starting from the late 1950s *italianità* became fashionable in America when a series of singers, actors, and sportsmen of Italian ancestry took the stage. But the *politics* behind that phenomenon was peculiarly American and had little to do with Italy. Frank Sinatra, Dick Martin, and Joe DiMaggio did not make Italians in Italy particularly proud, just like the mob movies of Scorsese, De Niro, and Pacino were hardly perceived as offensive by the Italian public. True, ethnic identity was, in fact, injected with a positive boost from the cache of cultural style and economic power coming from Italy. The prestige accorded Italy's cultural exports of films, fashion, and food did influence the re-evaluation of Italian/American identity as a positive construct.[27] Politically, however, that remained largely an Italian/American construct and provided no substitute for the missing link between the original fatherland and the Americanized, suburban middle class of Italian origin, which now constituted the backbone of that diasporic nation.

For post-war Italian Americans, Italy remains a distant, foreign land, a quasi-mythological point of reference. They seem to have developed a love-hate relationship with Italy, as many understandably rejected both ancient memories of misery and expulsion, and recollections of the "glorious twenty-year reign that lead to an inglorious war."

---

[27] This was the subject of the Calandra Institute's conference entitled The Three Fs in Italian Cultures: Critical Approaches to Food, Fashion, and Film (New York, April 28-30, 2011).

Post-war Italy, on the other hand, hardly provided itself, let alone its diasporic communities, with a new political discourse about national identity. The identification between Fascism and nationalism has made the Italian democratic republic the least "nationalistic," even the least "patriotic" country in Europe. So, when Aldo Grasso states in his interview quoted above that Italian Americans "understood the stereotype of one national identity [the Fascist one], but they have not gone through the process of understanding the next one [the republican one]," the reason may well be that the latter is weak in itself and very difficult to absorb, especially from abroad.

This also explains why some Italian Americans continue to "carry the rhetoric of Fascism with them." Indeed, when the "ethnic revival" of the 1970s made some form of identity politics again acceptable for Italian Americans, the nationalist-totalitarian rhetoric of Fascism re-emerged as the only known language through which "being Italian" could sound as something to be proud of and respected for. When old and new Italian/American associations came to the fore that was the language their leaders mostly used and understood.

On the one hand, it allowed them to again celebrate their mythological vision of *italianità* past and present, exhibiting their pride in Italy's contributions to world civilization as well as in what they had themselves given to America. On the other hand, it was a powerful rallying cry that could unite the community around its leaders. And it worked best when protesting discrimination and attacking the media industry that still looked at "Italians" through the lenses of working-class, uncultured, mob-like stereotypes.

Portraying Italian America as a glorious nation besieged by a hostile dominant culture and threatened by competing ethnic groups allowed ethno-nationalist elites to steer the Italian/American public discourse back to the totalitarian haven of propaganda celebrations and tireless anti-defamation censorship. And in this pre-modern warriors' refuge their perfectly legitimate power might last forever.[28]

---

[28] Although I am emphasizing here the Italian Fascist legacy on the Italian/American elite's

All this, of course, has no political meaning proper: looking at todays' Italian/American elites as a group of nostalgic neo-Fascists is perpetuating a nonsensical stereotype. They would look like ones *in Italy*—and indeed that is the self-deluding image that Italy's neo-Fascist party (the Movimento Sociale Italiano, later turned into Alleanza Nazionale, and finally merged into Berlusconi's Popolo della Libertà) has long tried to project. But in the U.S. they are as much loyal patriots and advocates of Americanization as they are fierce ethnic nationalists playing the card of Italian/American identity politics to advance their interests as self-appointed community leaders.

Back to the Future

In light of the above, it is understandable that Italian/American *prominenti* feel offended not only by the image of MTV's *Jersey Shore*, but even more by the very existence of guidos themselves. The latter represent a threat that comes from within the community, suggesting that some of their children do not fit with their propaganda image of Italian heritage, based on Dante and Columbus, Renaissance art, and opera. But, worst of all, the provocative guido lifestyle is unbearable to the *prominenti* as it risks to make people *laugh* at Italian Americans—the ultimate heresy indeed for those who live in what is ostensibly a pre-modern world. Within such a frame of mind, only one thing could be worse than the guido phenomenon, and it is a book (or an academic colloquium) about guido—for making a disturbing topic a legitimate object of scholarly inquiry is tantamount

rhetoric of identity, I am aware that this should be discussed within the broader framework of the "white backlash" in America. See Roger Hewitt, *White Backlash and the Politics of Multiculturalism* (Cambridge, Cambridge University Press, 2005). Such broadening of the scope of the analysis—which cannot even be attempted here—would also allow us to take into account the important phenomenon of Italian/American racism. See, for instance, Jerome Krase, "Bensonhurst, Brooklyn: Italian American Victims and Victimizers," in *The Review of Italian American Studies*, Frank M. Sorrentino and Jerome Krase, eds. (Lanham, Lexington Books, 2000) 233-44.

to accepting and legitimizing it. Hence, the chain reaction: from censoring the MTV show, to denying the existence of guido, to demanding that no "true" Italian/American intellectual engage in scholarly research or public discussion about it.

If all this shows anything, it is that in order to become a modern, civilized ethnic nation, Italian America needs to rid itself of a totalitarian-nationalist mindset and embrace a democratic-pluralist path to ethnic nation building. For this it needs, first of all, a new breed of intellectuals capable of progressive, critical, and even self-critical thinking—and perhaps of a little irony as well. Free, indeed, to write their books on any subject, without being asked to eat their own pages like a bunch of medieval censors. As suggested by the discussions published in this volume, the time may be ripe as a new generation of Italian American intellectuals is challenging older notions of identity politics and offering alternative visions.

Post scriptum

In the past seventeen years, Italy has been ruled—for the first time since World War II—by a political class that includes former neo-Fascist leaders and explicitly defines itself as "right-wing." Not surprisingly perhaps, these people's public discourse incorporated some elements reminiscent of the Italian/American anti-defamation rhetoric. Not only has Prime Minister Berlusconi repeatedly complained about best-selling Mafia-based books, movies, and TV shows that project the "wrong" image of Italy at home and abroad, but also the Speaker of the House, formerly the leader of the neo-Fascist party, has explicitly joined protests against *The Sopranos* while visiting the U.S. in 2009. This should come as no surprise: the newborn "nationalism" of Italy and the old "ethno-nationalism" of Italian America share the same roots in the censorship-and-propaganda rhetoric of Fascism. Both are, in a sense, modern-day caricatures of the grand nationalist-totalitarian discourse that Italy grew and exported before World War II. These similarities notwithstanding, most Italians in

Italy today still find it difficult to embrace the arguments put forward by Italian/American *prominenti*. Indeed, when in the winter 2010-2011, the Jersey Shore crew moved to the "fatherland" to shoot the new season's episode there—a very effective communication move targeted to the US public—few in Italy even noticed the horrified mournings coming from Italian/American headquarters.

1. Discussions

Real Italians
by Joseph Sciorra a.k.a. Joey Skee

When the self-appointed leaders of Italian America did what they do best—become insulted by media projections—it was evident that they were unaware of the existence of Italian-American youth in the northeast who self-ascribe as guidos. For these modern-day prominenti, *guido was only an ethnic epithet. Those of us from New York and the metropolitan area familiar with guido culture could only shake our heads in disbelief. Where had these "leaders" been for the past 30 years?*

We called them cugines. They were the super ginzos, the hyper wops, the swamp guineas. Deep, deep Brooklyn. We were Italian Americans, too, but different. Or so we wanted to be.

It wasn't the attention to hair, body, and cars that was troublesome at the time, but an ethnic identity directly linked to a geographically-bounded racism that I found ugly and frightening.

Located in the racially-charged neighborhood Canarsie, South Shore High School during the early 1970s was dictated by circumscribed groupings: Blacks and Puerto Ricans over there, whites over there. Several subdivisions existed among the white teenagers. Cugines and JAPs (Jewish American Princesses) were linked in a lower-middle-class, white ethnic style of puffy hair and disco. Freaks were dedicated to the American promise of sex (far too little), drugs (far too much), and rock 'n' roll (far too loud).

I straddled these different and often conflicting universes: a long-haired, bearded, salsa- and disco-dancing Italian American who desperately sought to escape the confines of his outer borough existence. Tony Manero riding the subway to Manhattan was a cinematic inspiration that helped motivate me to get the hell out.

Cugines morphed into guidos and ended up on *Jersey Shore*, and I got a PhD.

Of course, that's too simplistic an ending. My life is significantly more complicated than this truncated telling and so are those of guidos.

As a folklorist trained in ethnographic methodology and bridging the humanities and social sciences, I have spent the past thirty years researching the expressive cultures of Italian Americans in New York. I have often interviewed people whom I once labeled and dismissed as guidos, and who subsequently embraced the term as an ethnically-marked youth style.

It is fortunate that sociologist Donald Tricarico of Queensborough Community College, City University of New York has been studying guido culture for over twenty-five years. His scholarly investigation has helped me to understand and appreciate the varied ways expressivity and identity emerge among contemporary Italian Americans and, in particular, youth. (See the bibliography below.)

And then came MTV's reality show *Jersey Shore*.

When the self-appointed leaders of Italian America did what they do best—become insulted by media projections—it was evident that they were unaware of the existence of Italian-American youth in the northeast who self-ascribe as guidos. For these modern-day *prominenti*, guido was only an ethnic epithet. Those of us from New York and the metropolitan area familiar with guido culture could only shake our heads in disbelief. Where had these "leaders" been for the past thirty years?

Given this ostensible ignorance, I proposed that the John D. Calandra Italian American Institute invite Professor Tricarico to present his research on guido culture. He, in turn, suggested inviting Johnny DeCarlo to the academic colloquium, a northern New Jersey caterer and a self-professed guido with whom he communicated online.

Within two days of the Calandra Institute's email announcement for the event, Arthur Piccolo—"founder and chairman of the Bowling Green Association"—hurled a rambling invective against Professor Tricarico (the originally posted insult "MORON" was subsequently changed to "IDIOT"), Distinguished Professor Fred Gardaphé of Queens College, and the Calandra Institute in his January

7, 2010 blog post.[29] Piccolo's vituperation against "so called 'intellectuals'" states: "When in spite of their degrees and their titles they are nothing but dumb or worse traitors for a few pieces of silver thrown at them for pissing on their own community." Such a repugnant display of anti-intellectualism is as frightening as the many things I experienced during the 1970s among the cugines of South Shore High.

The January 21, 2010 colloquium Guido: An Italian-American Youth Style did not "glorify" guidos, as was the charge, any more than our previous lectures, readings, film screenings, and conferences have endorsed the Mafia, Fascism, anarchism, religion, Neapolitan music, neo-burlesque, or the other varied subjects presented at the Institute. Many of these self-professed leaders have rarely or never attended the Calandra Institute's free public events offered in midtown Manhattan. They were notably absent from the Calandra Institute's October 27, 2007 conference Recent Scholarship on Contemporary Italian-American Youth which featured Professor Tricarico's research on guidos. (I would be remiss not to mention that the National Italian American Foundation has supported the Calandra Institute with several generous grants.)

The appalling anti-intellectual reaction to the Calandra Institute colloquium raises some basic yet critical issues. What is Italian-American culture(s)? How is Italian-American identity reproduced? Who speaks for Italian Americans?

Anthropologist Fredrik Barth observed that ethnicity is a performance of difference displayed at the boundaries between groups. These ethnic borderlands are in constant flux, shifting from generation to generation, from moment to moment. Context is everything.

In addition, the "cultural stuff" that signifies *italianità* in the United States is constantly changing, yet a sense of Italian identity prevails. Being Italian American is not contingent on dancing the ta-

---

[29] Guido is another term for "Ginny" or "Wop" (www.italica.us/profiles/blogs/ guido-is-another-term-for).

rantella, eating spaghetti, or even speaking Italian. Hair gel or a dinner gala, in concert with other objects and behaviors, have come to signify "Italian" in certain contexts in what Professor Tricarico has called "a dynamic, adaptive character of ethnicity." Under what conditions does one object or activity become privileged over another as an expression of Italian-American identity?

Scholars have pointed out that Italian/American elites emerged as "power brokers," ethnic mediators positioned between the mass of Italian immigrants and mainstream American society. They served in this capacity by becoming arbitrators of what constitutes *italianità*. These *prominenti* historically devalued folk and vernacular expressions, promoting elite cultural forms like opera and establishing a pantheon of revered "ethnic heroes" like Columbus (see Harney 1993). Key to this work of cultural politics is the issue of "authenticity." What constitutes "real" Italian culture and "real" Italians? An annual gala dinner is no more an "authentic" expression of Italianness than hair gel, or, for that matter, speaking standard Italian. Individuals use these and other culturally-charged symbols to collectively shape meaning and create value as part of the varied expressions of Italian-American cultures and identities.

The Italian/American elite continues to have a vested interest in shaping and policing cultural expressions and ethnic identity. The late historian Philip Cannistraro, distinguished professor at Queens College and interim director of the Calandra Institute, noted:

> Throughout the Italian American experience, the *prominenti* have consistently endorsed a closely-linked agenda of "patriotism" and Americanization, which has essentially meant supporting the coercive efforts of American society designed to strip Italian immigrants and their descendants of their history, culture, and their identity. The dual focus of *prominentismo* has always been to promote the separate, self-aggrandizing interests of their own particular elite rather than of the community as a whole, and to stress what Italian Americans are not.

Cannistraro's historical assessment helps us put the most recent "controversy" concerning guidos in perspective: In whose interest is it to attack media representations, denigrate Italian-American youth, and stifle intellectual inquiry? Not mine.

Bibliography

Barth, Fredrik. 1969. "Introduction." *Ethnic Groups and Boundaries: The Social Organization of Culture Difference.* Fredrik Barth, Ed. (Boston: Little, Brown and Company. 9-38.

Cannistraro, Philip V. 2005. "The Duce and the Prominenti: Fascism and the Crisis of Italian of Italian American Leadership." *Altreitalie* (July-Dec.): 76-86.

Harney, Robert F. 1993. "Caboto and Other *Parentela*: The Uses of the Italian Canadian Past." *From the Shores of Hardship: Italians in Canada. Essays by Robert F. Harney.* Nicholas De Maria Harney, Ed. (Welland, ON: Éditions Soleil) 4-27.

Tricarico, Donald. 2008. "Dressing Italian Americans for the Spectacle: What Difference Does Guido Perform?" *The Men's Fashion Reader.* Andrew Reilly and Sarah Cosbey, Ed. (New York: Fairchild) 265-278.

——. 1991. "Guido: Fashioning an Italian American Youth Subculture." *The Journal of Ethnic Studies* (Spring): 41-66.

——. 2001. "Read All About It!: Representations of Italian Americans in the Print Media in Response to the Bensonhurst Racial Killing." *Notable Selections in Race and Ethnicity.* David V. Baker and Adalberto Aguirre, Jr., eds. (Sources, June): 291-319.

——. 2007. "Youth Culture, Ethnic Choice, and the Identity Politics of Guido." *VIA* 18.1 (Spring): 34-88.

Dialogue and Debate, Not Denigration and Dismissal
by Fred Gardaphé

Editors' Note: When some elements of the Italian/American community objected to the Calandra Institute holding the colloquium on guido culture, they singled out, among others, Professor Fred Gardaphé, for supporting the initiative and stating in a Time *magazine interview that the wave of negative response to* Jersey Shore *comes from what he calls "irony deficiency" in the Italian/American community. Here are Professor Gardaphé's responses to his critics.*

Dear Mr. ***,

I want to thank you for drawing attention through your recent blog[30] to the Calandra Institute's upcoming colloquium that was designed to investigate what is known as "guido" has been in existence for thirty years. Too often the Italian American community does not pay attention to the good work done at and through the Calandra Institute.

In that blog, Guido: The New Way to Mock Italian Americans, you say there are "so called 'intellectuals'... trapped by their own Bull Shit." I assume you are referring to me (for my statements reported in a *Time* magazine article[31]) and so I address this as my personal response to your claims.

I have never been referred to as a guido nor do I portray the behavior that might warrant such a characterization. First of all, you claim that what I say makes me "dumb" and "a traitor for a few pieces of silver" thrown my way. Such accusations are unfounded; I ask you here for a personal apology and a public withdrawal of those accusations. The work I do and have been doing for a good thirty years has never been funded by any insidious source that has enticed

---

[30] Guido is another term for "Ginny" or "Wop" (www.italica.us/profiles/blogs/ guido-is-another-term-for).

[31] Caryn Brooks, "Italian Americans and the G Word: Embrace or Reject?" Dec. 12, 2009 (time.com/time/nation/article/0,8599,1947338,00.html).

me to "betray" or even worse as you so crudely put it "piss on" my community.

On the contrary, my work has been motivated by my need to understand that community, and my responses to the exploration of that information have been the more than seven books I have written on the subject of the Italian American community. I have dedicated my professional life to this exploration, and your characterization of me is crude and could be construed as libelous. I have not garnered monetary wealth from this work and simply have a respected reputation that you have publicly attempted to defame. Your public apology would be greatly appreciated.

I don't believe that Donald Tricarico, as you say, "glorifies guido." Tricarico is a sociologist who has spent time trying to understand aspects of the larger Italian American community that are often manipulated by the media. Guido culture is not something the media created; in fact, Italian American culture, for better or worse, has created guido culture, and that I believe is something that must be investigated and understood before we can move further in any discussion. Dr. Tricarico, as any good social scientist, describes guido culture for those who are interested. He doesn't "Love it" or "Hate it."

I can understand your anger and your fear at the recent dominance of this culture's representation in the media. Once again, a small segment of the Italian American population is getting the attention that the major part of Italian American culture has never respectfully received. This has been one of the greatest problems that our community has faced, and one that we hope to address through intellectual investigation and through the promotion of alternative artistic and media works. This has been the foundation of what has been produced by the Calandra Institute since its inception and one of the reasons I was drawn to my current affiliation.

I find the Calandra Institute's wording of this upcoming colloquium to be accurate and appropriate. Guido culture is something that is "non-traditional" and represents the way a number of Americans of Italian descent have chosen to identify themselves as being Italian American. No one ever said they represent the whole of the culture, and actually, within Dr. Tricarico's work, you will find the information you need to more cogently critique what you see as a negative representation of Italian American culture.

Whatever it is one feels about guido culture, all Italian Americans share some responsibility for having created it. Whether those inside guido culture have created their identities out of arrogant animosity toward what some consider to be traditional representations of Italian American culture—both within and without the Italian community—or through some interpretation based on attentive admiration of publicly presented versions of Italian American culture, what needs to be examined is just what is and what isn't Italian or American about guido culture, and what is or isn't of our own creation. That is what I feel is the work at hand.

I have many students who feel that guido culture does not represent them, the same way that most Italian Americans feel that gangster culture does not reflect them. I also have students who feel comfortable within versions of guido culture. This is simply a reality that such a colloquium will enable us to examine.

I have never once publicly applauded the MTV television program that has brought attention back to this culture, and I do not accept your interpretation of a recent misquoting of my response to one reporter as enthusiastic support of it. In fact, I simply said that it is just more of what MTV has been throwing out for years without much protest from other communities. The reporter mistook my interpretation of *guappo* for guido and that's where some of the confusion might lie.

I do believe strongly in there being an irony deficiency within some members of the Italian American community that does not allow them to connect to the more artistic misrepresentations of Italian America that appear in the arts. I never said irony deficiency was a right or wrong thing; those are your words. I simply identified it and have been working to document it and explain it, much the same way Dr. Tricarico has worked to document and interpret guido culture.

That guidos take pride in themselves is no reason to encourage "young Italian boys and girls" to join them. Such reasoning would lead to the suggestion that the First Amendment is at the root of all this representative evil.

I think this colloquium is a great opportunity for all Americans to better understand all sides of this issue. By calling for a boycott, or even worse a cancellation, of this colloquium you are not only denying the right of free speech, but also the necessity of intellectual investigation of all aspects of the community. It is imperative that we debate intelligently and respectfully all issues, whatever we may think of them. I find this quite sad and little more than a reminder that the generation gaps inside Italian America will continue to grow and remain unbridged.

Professor Tricarico does not need any "proof" of his credibility; but we all need to consider his research as we attempt to fashion powerful ways of addressing Italian American identities today and for the future. I hope you, as well as others who might consider not attending, will reconsider and join us for what promises to be a significantly informative, and thus beneficial discussion for all.

Sincerely,
F.G.

* * *

Dear Mr. ***,

I'm glad that this controversy has brought our voices and ideas into conversation. For too long our community has kept business separate from intellectual pursuit. I believe you, like most Italian Americans, are not familiar with the work that I have produced over the last thirty years and perhaps this interaction will result in a greater awareness of the work I and many others have produced. Many of us have spent our lives examining the phenomenon of Italian immigration to the United States with the purpose of understanding and improving the lot of the Italian American. Communication between us can help improve our community by promoting the sharing of knowledge and resources in pursuit of better lives.

We agree on many things and so I suggest we base the foundation of our discussions on that and then debate that upon which we do not agree. I would never challenge another person's beliefs and so agree with you that Mr. Piccolo is "not wrong in his beliefs." You are right that "we should be joining forces and begin attacking the problem." This initial colloquium is part of making that happen. By framing the problem and examining it from various angles we will be better able to formulate strategies for solutions.

Politicians usually arm themselves with studies conducted by academic think tanks and perhaps that's what's been the problem with our politicians. When the Calandra Institute provided our politicians with the information about the Italian American dropout rate those politicians rallied to solve that problem. Would this have been done if someone had said the Institute should spend more time promoting the positive instead of investigating drop-outs? Cancer never was a good thing, and when people started studying it we started finding solutions. And if we don't study the phenomena of our own community, then we are left with reacting to what the news and entertainment media present.

This colloquium, one of many the Calandra Institute has offered since its inception, is not focused on the MTV television show, rather the culture that the show purports to represent. Who better to give us insight into just what the fuss is all about than a social scientist who has actually studied the subculture for many years? This colloquium is a signal to the world that we are taking control of our own representations. This colloquium is not the first nor will it be the last word on this subject. A few years ago the Calandra did a similar colloquium on youth culture at Queens College and not one Italian American organization responded to it.

My students at Queens College will be hosting a roundtable in the spring on Italian American youth lifestyles that will be part of a larger series on Italian American youth culture. Through these events we hope for all to gain a better understanding of what is happening to those who will someday take over the leadership of our community. This is why it is so important that all of our leaders should plan on attending these and other events. I must say that when I was their age, a while ago, no one in the Italian community paid attention to my attempts to forge an Italian American identity, which I did through many successful and unsuccessful attempts.

Let's make this the beginning of better interaction among leaders in the business, social, educational, and cultural institutions of Italian America. Combining the brains, brawn, and beauty of our community can only help us all no matter where we work or live.

I hope that with the support of leaders such as yourself we can begin to work together to better understand what it meant, means, and will mean to be Italian Americans.

Sincerely,
F.G.

Guidos and Negros
by Jerry Krase

The Italian and Italian-American traditions share many common practices, the most important of which for the case at hand is the knack for rhetorical and other displays. It is the "others," such as WASPs, who are supposed to be tight-lipped and uptight when it comes to potentially embarrassing issues. In my opinion, the term guido and its associated youth style deserves a coolheaded discussion, as well as the heated conversation it now enjoys.

It is with great reluctance and intense trepidation that I enter into the—excuse the term—"passionate" debate, or rather heated argument, about whether either ordinary people, such as myself, or professors, such as myself, have the God (G-d, Allah)-given, or United States Constitution-given right to use all words when I talk about the discourse-defined world in which I currently reside.

So here goes: "Guinea, Dago, Wop, Greaseball, Ginzo, Guido, Italian-American, American of Italian descent, Italo-American, Italian/American," are all verbal expressions of varying degrees of insult/pride that have been used to stand for those people whom it can be claimed, or who claim for themselves, a cultural/genetic heritage that is traceable to, more or less, the real or imagined boundaries of a place called "Italy." To equivocate, but only somewhat: "Nigger, Negro, Colored, African-American, Afro-American, Black, Person of Color" are all verbal expressions of varying degrees of insult/pride that have been used to stand for those people whom it can be claimed, or who claim for themselves, a cultural/genetic heritage that is traceable to, more or less, the real or imagined boundaries of a place called "Africa."

When I was a child growing up in the yet (1940s and '50s) majority peopled White-European low-income Red Hook housing project in Brooklyn, my mother once washed out my mouth with soap for using the N-word, and I didn't get to hear the G-word uttered as an epithet until I discovered its quotidian employment in common teenage F-word-laden conversations along with "Mocky," "Spic," and "Mick" for Jews, Puerto Ricans, and Irish dis/respectively. The fact that the gang with which I was associated contained authentic members of each of these varieties of be-pimpled ethnics, including Ns, was, as today, no *prophylaxis* from political incorrectness (RCs, please excuse the offensive term, but it is not as bad as "ejaculation" that I found lurking in a pamphlet about indulgences). To be fair, I must also note that we, Catholics, were referred to as "Mackerel Snappers" by anti-papist, heathen Protestants as mutual speechified bigotry was rampant but hardly noticed in those halcyon days.

Getting back to the point, "Congress shall make no law respecting an establishment of religion, or prohibiting the free exercise thereof; or abridging the freedom of speech, or of the press; or the right of the people peaceably to assemble, and to petition the Government for a redress of grievances." There have been, over the last two centuries, many seemingly reasonable restrictions placed on these fragments of the Bill of Rights, and post-9/11 abridgments have been popping up like poison mushrooms all around us. The biggest threats, however, to our cherished freedoms of expressions as, for, and by Italian Americans seem to come from other Italian Americans.

It is ironic that Harry Reid, accurately discussing the racism that infects American political discourse at every level, is called a "racist" for, in part, correctly and in/sensitively using the term Negro in a candid analysis of then presidential candidate Barack Hussein Obama's likelihood of getting through the complexion/dialect test that was tougher for him than riding a camel (excuse the Saharan animal reference) through the eye of the needle, so to speak. Similarly, my good friends and colleagues Donald Tricarico and Fred Gardaphé (and I) have (more than once) been taken to task by the ethnic pride/thought police for saying things they feel should be left unsaid. In the current case of having one's underwear in a bunch, it is guidos of one or another kind and, as was true with attempts to prohibit even the faintest praise of things Soprano-esque, the attacks can only serve, sadly, to focus more attention on both another crappy MTV "reality" program and, happily, the problem of Italian American ethnic stereotyping that continues to impact all of "us" (excuse my inclusion in the aggrieved class).

Not all stereotypes are negative but all stereotypes can have negative effects. There have been many images of Italians held in the minds of Americans. In the earliest years, Italians were esteemed as passionate, artistic, learned, liberal, and skilled. By the turn of the 20th century the image had been almost totally transformed by the "tired, poor, and huddled masses," except for the passionate bits. By the turn of the 21st century the passion had dissipated somewhat, and some Italian Americans even became icons of exceptional, positive "American" values such as home and family. Unfortunately, one of the most persistent stereotypes is of Italian Americans as anti-intellectual, crude, rude, and thuggish. In this regard, I think Italian Americans have every right, and good reason, to protest the frequent media depiction of some of the "lifestyles" that are presented as though they were intrinsically Italian as opposed to being bad cultural choices open to all.

The latest version of hot-button media stereotyping is of the guido style. The word has been around for quite some time but for those who practice it, it is hardly related to its historically offensive source. I know many Italian American and non-Italian American young men who sport one or another aspect of the style, also referred to (still, I believe) as cugine at some of the clubs I never frequented. Some of my best ... are ... but, I am a cultural/style curmudgeon, and personally, I don't get the guido-appeal as it's not aimed at me. For example, when, other than catchers, people began wearing their baseball caps backwards, I was appalled and railed about it in front of my young children as, liberal political icon, New York City Mayor David Dinkins engaged in what I considered that "ghetto" practice; and when their ethnically varied boyfriends came into the house thusly garbed, I had all I could do to keep myself from snide comment. Today disgraced Wall Street executives wear their Yankees caps like the mayor they couldn't bring themselves to vote for. Maybe someday they will become guidos and guidettes.

Some argue that the agency of youth created the style, such as when Buckwheat's *Our Gang* pickaninny ensemble became couture; especially of pants that (in my opinion) didn't fit and which has unfortunately (again in my opinion) been emulated by white as well as black style hounds. To me, thusly everyone looks stupid, which I guess is a condition of stereotypical equality/equity. I associate the guido style with excessive preening and narcissism, but then again, when I was a handsome young, muscular teenager, constantly combing my Vaseline-slicked back DA (duck's ass) haircut, I, and the (excuse the word) girls thought it was "cool." My exceedingly tight pants and muscleman T-shirts were also "tough guy" de rigueur in my neighbor-"hood." Upon reflection, I looked like a "hood" but would hardly be called a Mafia-type or a guido as I had no idea at the time that my mother's family came from Sicily. If I did, it might have made a difference. Perhaps I would have been, like the half-Italian Henry Hill, initiated into the local Italian (as opposed to Irish or Jewish) mob. Mine, ensconced near the 80th Precinct made in/famous by the Knapp Commission, was, after all, only a block away. I doubt if the young men and women who relish their *guidità* today are of much danger except to themselves and those who, for whatever reason, seem to be fascinated by their real/virtual exploits.

It still is true that Italian Americans suffer from both irony deficiency as well as bad press, but it won't be cured by attacks on, for example, the John D. Calandra Italian American Institute that over the years has raised the level of respect for Italian America by providing a place for top-notch Italian American scholars and scholarship. Italian-American scholars (as well as "half-ones") have had a great deal of difficulty getting proper recognition from their professional peers for their Italo-work in part because "ethnic studies" in general is seen as a "lesser" academic pursuit characterized by filiopietism and ethnic boosterism. Ethnic chauvinism, it is true, taints much of the output in these fields, but it is mainly because practitioners are often dependent on the largesse of the communities in question and therefore skirt "difficult" issues such as racial, ethnic, and gender biases, among other afflictions.

New York State Senator John D. Calandra expended a great deal of his hard-won political capital in fostering higher education for, and objective research on, Italian Americans. To limit reasonable consideration of any issue in and about Italian Americans would be an insult to his foundational enterprise. As with so many other things ethnic, there are those within the Italian American community who traffic in the negatives (and positive) stereotypes, but Professors Donald Tricarico and Fred Gardaphé are well outside that pale. I wasn't intending on going to Guido: An Italian-American Youth Style on Thursday, January 21 from 10:00 a.m. to noon at the John D. Calandra Italian American Institute, 25 West 43rd Street, 17th floor (between 5th and 6th Avenues) in Manhattan, which is free and open to the public, but seating is limited so please call (212) 642-2094 to pre-register and also be prepared to show a photo ID to the building's concierge, however I will come as a show of solidarity with all those who understand how important academic, as well as artistic, freedom of expression is in today's society.

The Situation
by Robert Viscusi

Guido is a phenomenon that demands attention. If Italian American social ad-
vance were as real, as secure, and as substantial as many Italian Americans believe
it to be (I am among these believers), then it would seem not only not harmful, but
indeed positively beneficial and necessary, to examine, to discuss, and to reflect
upon the power of such a new word.

As to the youths of Jersey Shore, they are playing grotesques, like all minstrel-
show caricatures. They are amusing—indeed, more so than most clowns with sad
eyes. They have clearly found their moment and clearly touched a nerve. To the
term Italian American, which has carried so many strings of dollar bills and ropes
of sausage, they have added a new chain of fetishes—a tanning bed, a tube of gel,
an old summer thong bearing the legend "I Love the Situation."

Jersey Shore is an MTV reality show that follows eight housemates, aged 22 through 29, spending their summer living together in a house in Seaside Heights, New Jersey. Young adults simultaneously trying and refusing to grow up, they live a life characterized by self-contradiction and cross-purposes. As is so often the case in reality television, the mating rituals of consumerist society, brutal and even grotesque, are placed on view, as are the prepackaged sensitivity rituals among the participants, who try to sympathize with one another's wounds even as they conspire to objectify, sexualize, and humiliate one another and themselves as well, pretty much all day and all night, sometimes even when sleeping.

All of this is predictable enough. Reality TV, with its mingling of the minstrel show and the slave market, has been the most popular form of TV in the United States for the past ten years—*Survivor, American Idol, America's Next Top Model,* to use only the most obvious examples, have been steady favorites, continually generating conversation at water coolers and on talk shows.

Jersey Shore belongs to that world of conversation. Why do people talk about it?

First and foremost, the characters are notable for the rituals of self-care that define them.

Snooki, a 21-year-old from Marlboro, New York, has her own tanning bed. She wears her hair in a pouf reminiscent of the hairdresser styles of the late '50s and early '60s.

DJ Pauly D also owns a tanning bed. He spends twentyfive minutes a day applying gel to his hair to produce an effect that girls will want to touch.

JWoww is a 23-year-old club promoter whose 21st birthday present to herself was a breast augmentation, whose effects she dresses to emphasize.

Mike calls himself "The Situation." The assistant manager of a fitness center in Staten Island, he boasts remarkably emphatic "abs." He calls them "The Situation" because they produce strong interest. He works in a T-shirt shop where he sells thongs that bear, across the crotch, the legend "I Love the Situation."

The four other characters, Angelina, Sammi "Sweetheart," Ronnie, and Vinny are all similarly devoted to degrees of physical culture and self-advertisement, but not quite so dramatically as the first four.

Determined, even obsessive, rituals of self-presentation belong to the slave-market aspect of the show, a feature it shares with many other popular forms of spectacle—modeling contests, talent competitions, beauty pageants—where the performers burnish their secondary sexual characteristics, hoping to attract prizes or at least buyers. Snooki, for example, dresses like a showgirl, and JWoww displays the perfect domes of her enhanced bosoms, but both occasionally profess their desires to make careers, not as hookers or showgirls, but as wives of guidos. As Snooki puts it, "My ultimate dream is to move to Jersey, find a nice juiced hot tanned guy and live my life."[32]

There is something incredibly old-fashioned about the ambitions of these souped-up young bodies. And that brings us to the other,

---

[32] http://www.jerseyshorequotes.com/cast/snooki_quotes.htm

more controversial aspect of the series: its minstrel-show representation of Italian Americans. Here is the most provocative statement of the theme, uttered by DJ Pauly D:

> I was born and raised a Guido. It's just a lifestyle. It's about being Italian. It's representing family, friends, tanning, gel, everything. Dude I got a fucking tanning bed in my place, that's how serious I am about being a guido and living up to that lifestyle. My tagline is 'I'm Your Girl's Favorite DJ.' I want the Guidettes to come in their pants when they hear my music.[33]

There are viewers whose response to this kind of statement has the eyeblink speed of a conditioned reflex. There have been two levels of protest.

The first is very general, and very familiar in nature. Many Italian American organizations have joined this protest. Andrè DiMino, president of UNICO National, says the show "sends the wrong message. This type of programming represents a direct affront and attack by MTV on the character of Italian Americans, the fourth-largest ethnic group in America."[34] The Order Sons of Italy in America and the National Italian American Foundation have taken similar positions, calling on MTV to take the show off the air. This response is hardly surprising; nor, in the general marketplace of ethnic stereotypes, is it out of place. Italian American civic organizations, devoted to supporting the social advance of Italian Americans, must respond this way when anyone presents the identity *Italian American* in a way that causes it to lose what they perceive as social value and/or prestige. In the days of *The Godfather* and *The Sopranos*, these organizations took similar positions.

The protest has the character of a class defense. Italian Americans are rising in the world. Doctors, lawyers, writers, professors, Supreme Court Justices, the Speaker of the House, corporation pre-

---

[33] http://www.inkandbeans.com/2009/12/best-quotes-from-premiere-of-mtvs.html
[34] http://iaonevoice.blogspot.com/2009/11/mtv-shore-show-slurs-ia-community.html

sidents and CEOs—pillars of respectability abound. *Jersey Shore*, though it does not feature gangsters, ignores all this movement in the direction of quiet refinement. Rather, it brings the meaning of the expression *Italian American* back to the world of the working class, where beauty is all on the surface, and long-range consequences, so beloved of the upwardly-mobile, have nothing to do with it. The stars of *Jersey Shore* are not interested in delayed gratification. Their position is made firmly clear by Snooki, speaking on the *Wendy Williams Show*:

> The Italian, whatever, national, whatever their organization is, they don't understand that guidos and guidettes are good-looking people that, you know, like to make a scene and be center of attention and just take care of themselves.... [These national organizations] are old-fashioned. They don't know that; they think it's offensive, because maybe in their time it was offensive, but now it's kind of a compliment. So they don't understand that and that is what we are trying to say. They are way overreacting to the show. We're 22 to 29 just having fun at the shore. They are just taking it way out of proportion.[35]

To which the leaders of Italian American organizations might reply, "Fine. Enjoy yourselves. Just understand that you are defaming a brand name that we share with you." And of course they are right. The entry of Italian Americans into elite social groups has not kept pace with their academic and economic achievements. For example, 4.6 percent of college professors are Italian American, a portion close to the Italian American presence (5.6 percent) in the general population. But the Italian American presence in the American Academy of Arts and Sciences, the leading elite intellectual group in the nation, is 1.3 percent, a figure suggestive of the unspoken barriers and diminished value that still attaches to their shared identification.[36]

---

[35] http://www.usmagazine.com/moviestvmusic/news/italian-american-alyssa-milano-mtvs-jersey-shore-upset-me-20091112

[36] Richard Alba and Dalia Abdel-Hardy, "Galileo's Children: Italian Americans' Difficult

58

What shall we make of problems like this? The John D. Calandra Italian American Institute of the City University of New York, whose mission and goals include "heightening awareness, fostering higher education, and conducting research to deepen understanding of Italian Americans' culture and heritage," announced a lecture and discussion on Guido: An Italian-American Youth Style to be led by Donald Tricarico, a sociologist and author who has studied this subculture, and by Johnny DeCarlo, a self-identified guido. It would seem appropriate to have a serious discussion of something that many Italian Americans see as a serious threat to their social advance.

But no.

Instead, this event brings us to the second level of protest. A wide variety of persons has protested the presentation of this colloquium. Arthur Piccolo, writing on italica.us, takes the line that the very term guido is so offensive that it ought never to be uttered, much less studied and discussed, by an Italian American, not even a scholar trained to analyze social facts. Piccolo gets so angry about this that he writes, "Meet Dr. Donald Tricarico who regardless of his ancestry does not deserve to be called an Italian American."[37] Piccolo, like many others, attributes a peculiar negative power to the word.

It is not easy to disagree with him, but it is also necessary to do so. For the word guido has a complex meaning, and to read it as having a simple valence, negative or positive, is to miss the eloquence of the phenomenon it represents. Guido is a word in process of transvaluation, according to Donald Tricarico. "Guido is a slur, but Italian kids have embraced it just as Black kids have embraced the N— word. In the same way that radical gays call themselves queer."[38]

Entry into the Intellectual Elite," *The Sociological Quarterly* 46 (2005) 3-18.
[37] http://iaonevoice.blogspot.com/2009/11/mtv-shore-show-slurs-ia-community.html
[38] http://www.time.com/time/nation/article/0,8599,1947338,00.html# ixzz0d5Fq75Co.

In fact, the entire ensemble of guido behaviors presents Italian American culture in a funhouse mirror, with meanings distorted and turned upside down. The emphasis on virginity and female virtue in the traditional Italian American family recurs here in the caricature of maternal abundance in the florid display of copious mammaries and child-bearing hips. Angelina says, "I have real boobs. I have a nice, fat ass."[39] Given her name, it is not difficult to see her as advertising herself as a candidate for Italian American wedlock and motherhood.

Is it too far-fetched to see in this working-class culture a powerful force of nostalgic (i.e., home-seeking) behavior, Southern Italians who seek out their ancestral and stereotypical darkness with tanning beds in their rooms, into which they lay themselves down like Orpheus descending into the underworld, farmers' grandchildren who exaggerate their fertility with their grotesque miming of sexuality, 21st century breeding partners still looking for simple fidelity to an ethnic identity that, in practice, they often do not know how to achieve. Two of the most feverish mate-hunters among them, Snooki and Pauly D, spend much of their time pursuing partners who are, respectively, Irish, and Israeli. Guido, with its double value, positive and negative, is a term flexible enough to represent an Italian American identity that both is and isn't something in particular.

The level of linguistic inventiveness and of cultural improvisation present here is evident not only in the words but in the stunning remarks that emerge from the characters' mouths.

> JWoww: I am like a praying mantis, after I have sex with a guy I will rip their heads off.[40]
>
> Sammi Sweetheart: Go home. You don't belong here. You don't even look Italian![41]
>
> Mike "The Situation": G.T.L. baby. Gym, Tanning, Laundry.[42]

---

[39] http://www.inkandbeans.com/2009/12/best-quotes-from-premiere-of-mtvs.html

[40] http://www.jerseyshorequotes.com/cast/j-woww_quotes.htm

[41] http://www.jerseyshorequotes.com/cast/sammi_quotes.htm

Vinny: These kids are robots... Gym, Tanning, Laundry... that's how they make the guidos. I don't follow those rules at all... I can see if it was Basketball, Pool, Beach.[43]

It is the wit of people living in a borderland, negotiating the need to seem certain even when nothing can be ascertained.

This is a phenomenon that demands attention. If Italian American social advance were as real, as secure, and as substantial as many Italian Americans believe it to be (I am among these believers), then it would seem not only *not* harmful, but indeed positively beneficial and necessary, to examine, to discuss, and to reflect upon the power of such a new word. Are we mature enough, sensible enough, secure enough in our sense of our own inheritance, to engage in such reflection? I want merely to point out that the achievement of high social and intellectual status in the United States requires that we look firmly at the things we most instinctively dislike and fear about our selves, both internally and externally.

Internally, we need to ask, have we really distanced ourselves from our working-class roots so little that the very signs of these roots, appearing on a television show, must enrage and disgust us? And if so, why?

Externally, we need to ask, do we need to be responsive and responsible to every person that tries to define our relationship with our inherited identities? If I am Italian American, is it not within my power to write about that in my own way, in terms that no one else needs to use or accept?

As to the youths of *Jersey Shore*, they are playing grotesques, like all minstrel-show caricatures. They are amusing—indeed, more so than most clowns with sad eyes. They have clearly found their moment and clearly touched a nerve. To the term *Italian American*, which has carried so many strings of dollar bills and ropes of sausage, they have

---

[42] http://www.jerseyshorequotes.com/cast/the-situation_quotes.htm
[43] http://www.jerseyshorequotes.com/cast/vinny_quotes.htm

added a new chain of fetishes—a tanning bed, a tube of gel, an old summer thong bearing the legend "I Love the Situation."

Stereotype, Caricature, or Lifestyle?
by Chiara and Franco Montalto

What is this guido thing? Is it pure caricature put on us by the outside world, or do we have an active part in it? Is it lifestyle and stylistic choice or demeaning stereotype? A (former guido) brother who now teaches environmental engineering and a (longtime anti-guido) sister who is now an actress, writer, and filmmaker look back.

I am the anti-guido/ette. I'm very proud to have never, ever had big hair. Though when my brother Franco and I were growing up in the late '80s and early '90s, he (and everyone else, it seemed) at the time was a guido. Personally, I wanted *nothing* to do with the world of Z. Cavaricci, gold chains, and big, sprayed and gelled hair, and loud, obnoxious dance music.

An introverted and overly sensitive kid, by the age of 10, I was interested in and pained by apartheid in South Africa and other problems in faraway places, and these things seemed to me to be a universe away from the loud music my brother blasted from his room, and the dance clubs he frequented on the weekends. I escaped into a private world of books, artists, and music by the Cure, U2 and eventually Nirvana, what I considered the ultimate anti-guido band. When my mother referred to me as a mix of Morticia Adams, Frida Kahlo and Sylvia Plath, she wasn't really that far off base.

Neither my brother nor I turned out half bad. He went on to go to Cooper Union, become a Fulbright scholar, and, ultimately got his PhD in environmental engineering from Cornell. Now, he is a professor of environmental engineering at Drexel University, and with his Black, Barbados-born, Brooklyn-raised wife, Sharon, has two kids, Simona and Nicolò. I emerged from my shell to become an actress, writer, and filmmaker, and work as a paralegal to make ends meet.

When we reflect back on our adolescence, my brother says he feels no shame. He views his "guido years" as a stylistically expressed cultural choice that helped him feel like he belonged somewhere during the always difficult teenage years. My brother looks back on his guido years with fondness and nostalgia. It was a phase that helped him to develop self-respect, an independent and bold spirit, and, importantly, compassion for others who are portrayed in an unflattering way by the mainstream. Somewhere, I know he's still got that purple Cavaricci suit that made him look like a gigantic grape.

Which is why, twenty years later, I'm surprised to find myself writing about the latest guido-centered phenomenon—MTV's *Jersey Shore*. Let's face it, this is reality television, folks. It's the car accident and we're all rubbernecking. Personally, I don't look to this stuff for its artistic merit. It is television product that's created to do one thing: get maximum exposure and publicity with a minimum of cost. At that, MTV has succeeded, greatly. Are there messed up, offensive images in this and other shows? Yes, no question.

Are there stereotypical images of Italian Americans in mainstream media? Absolutely. As a professional actress, I'm rarely called in for non-stereotypical Italian-American roles. I hear it all the time: "You are very *specific looking*," whatever that means. Maybe if there wasn't an audience eager to gobble this stuff up like candy, to rubberneck at the aforementioned car accident, we'd all be a little further on down the road.

I asked my brother recently to define the word guido. He told me it wasn't a term that he and his friends used. He felt it was coined by the mainstream to describe a group of people who sought to distinguish themselves in a distinct way, because they actually *felt* different, yet also felt they could not express their otherness freely in public, without enduring some kind of ridicule. What he was is not what they thought he was.

Further, he feels some of the guidos *were* in fact, different: their parents and grandparents spoke or had knowledge of other languages, were dark in complexion, may not have been educated, had names that were hard to pronounce, considered family and close friends as the only people who could really be trusted, lived in houses full of bleeding-heart crucifixes, plastic fruit, glasses of wine at dinner, and other objects used to express pride of economic successes in the new country. The awareness of the presence of some of these things in his life, and the associated awareness of their lacking in the lives of some of his peers, significantly affected his adolescent quest to define his own personal identity. In a pluralistic society, these kinds of reactions are normal. In college, I read Dick Hebdige's *Subculture: The Meaning of Style* in which he essentially makes the same point, though his analysis is of Rastafarians and punks. I'd suggest that book be read by those with a strong opinion on this matter.

Several years ago, I took a class taught by Dr. Joe Sciorra at the John D. Calandra Italian American Institute on the everyday performance of Italian-Americans. It was at the height of *The Sopranos* controversy, and I had been, up until that point, pretty anti-Sopranos. (I also didn't have HBO, but that was another matter.) In class, we analyzed the Columbus Day episode of *The Sopranos* and I discovered that it was the *only* show on TV trying to capture the various levels of dispute and discord within the Italian American community about Columbus Day. That class totally changed the way I looked at things.

The Calandra Institute will be holding a colloquium on January 21 to look at the guido culture. Is the guido simply a stereotype, or is there more there, lurking under the surface? Scholars, writers, academics, professors, and folklorists are looking, studying, and discussing, as they should be.

So here we are, opening up this idea for discussion, taking the lid off the Pandora's box of Italian American identity. What is this guido thing? Is it pure caricature put on us by the outside world, or do we play an active part? Is it lifestyle or demeaning stereotype? If, in fact, it is a subculture as defined by Hebdige, then what does that mean for Italian-Americans' current place in modern American society? Are we still viewed as outsiders? The Calandra Institute and its symposium offer a place to start this discussion. I'm no expert and certainly not an academic, but I know that by opening up this dialogue in this forum, we are taking the first step towards transcending stereotypes and defining our own place in American society. And yet there are those who would rather this colloquium not take place, that this Pandora's box just not be opened. They'd rather sweep this all under the proverbial rug and go on pretending that the beginning and end of the Italian American experience is red sauce on a Sunday afternoon. *Bella figura* at its best, or maybe at its worst. To those people, I say, though change is never easy, when you change the way you look at things, the things you look at change.

On Guidos, Gramsci, and Irony Deficiency
by Laura E. Ruberto

Why Italian Americans need to take action, a Pasquinian response to some recent debates.

In response to recent posts on i-Italy, Facebook, the H-ItAm list-serv, and elsewhere regarding *Jersey Shore* and the Calandra Institute's upcoming colloquium on guido culture, I have been asked by the i-Italy editors to chime in.

This topic brings to the surface broader concerns and the need of influential community leaders to help make a change. I'm talking about the need for more old-fashioned, organic intellectuals—the kind that would make Antonio Gramsci feel all warm and fuzzy inside.

I've come up with a short list of some issues concerning Italian Americans I think could be changed for the better with the help of proper intellectual guidance and earnest debate:

- We need more *paesani* on the highest court in the land. Regard-less of their politics, the fact that there are only two Italian American Supreme Court Justices suggests Italian Americans en masse are not being taken seriously.
- MTV, HBO, or any other media outlet should not be allowed to create shows that depict Italian Americans, past or present. I don't care so much about depictions of Italians as Mafiosi or guidettes (after all, here in California no one knows what the difference is anyway); I'm just plain annoyed when they get some cultural detail wrong. I mean, what if there's a wedding scene and they forget the cookies? *Che vergogna!*
- We should be hostile to cultural or political references that con-nect contemporary immigration to Italy (think of the recent events in Calabria) with Italy's history of emigration. Italians have no-thing in common with the immigrants who live and work in Italy today; such comparisons are ludicrous! And why, why should we believe Dennis Hopper anyway?

-   In fact, we should discourage education generally, and seriously reconsider censorship. It might be time to bring back "red squads"—but rather than focus on communists (way too retro) they could infiltrate any institution that is trying to promote critical thought, dialogue, or debate.

Ma dai! Who would get behind such nonsense?

But let's return to my man, Gramsci. Now, Gramsci—yes, I am in all earnestness, citing that rabble-rousing radical—figured most folks were already set in their ways and thus realized that unless some people started looking at the world a little differently, no cultural transformation (an alternative national popular culture, if you will), could possibly happen:

> No mass action is possible, if the masses in question are not convinced of the ends they wish to attain and the methods to be applied.
>
> (Gramsci, *The Southern Question*)

And how better to get to that common ground than to hear from informed and well-trained scholars as well as listen to people's real-life experiences and points of view?

It seems to me that getting people talking and thinking critically about themselves, the media, and the development of culture generally is certainly something that would make Gramsci raise his glass.

And this is the kind of action I'm interested in talkin' about.

(My posts on i-italy.org typically consist of "notes," toned-down academic sketches for ideas I may later develop in more traditional scholarly contexts. In this topical piece, however, I took a somewhat different tack: while I invoke such recherche figures as Pasquino, a Roman symbol of the public lampoon, and Antonio Gramsci, the Sardinian leftist philosopher and political activist, my main concern was to fire off a defense—in what I hope is suitably tongue-in-cheek style—of some of my New York colleagues' efforts to create a public scholarly venue for discussion of popular media representations of so-called guido culture. My entreaty for insightful debate and inquisitive scholarship was earnest, but my tone was calculatedly breezy and ironic. Beyond the irony is a call for critical distancing and a global perspective that recognizes the real lives of immigrants in relation to dominant culture.)

Organized Culture
by Fred Gardaphé

If you believe that Jersey Shore on MTV is really gangsters without guns, then you should do something about it. But since when have we become afraid of our youth? Since when has the public behavior of seven 20-something kids been something to pay attention to? This shows that kids don't really know what it means to be Italian American outside of their family; it also shows that we probably don't know our kids as well as we think we do. So don't blame MTV; we have failed ourselves.

We may think we have created Italian America, but we have yet to create Italian Americans.

Italian Americans have been formally complaining about the way they have been portrayed in the media since as far back as 1931 with little or no effect. That year, Fiorello LaGuardia, then mayor of New York City, wrote a letter to William H. Hays, the first president of the Motion Picture Producers and Distributors of America, to protest the portrayal of Italians in the film *Little Caesar*. Obviously nothing has changed, yet over the same 80-year period, other racial and ethnic American groups such as Jewish Americans and African Americans have succeeded in changing the way their images have been presented. So what's the difference?

Lately, I have attended a couple of so-called summits organized by a national organization (of which I am a member) and a group of local people in lower Manhattan. I have listened to the best of what all the speakers had to say and can only say that nothing new was offered. Protests were suggested, and while that might work for the powerful, showing up with dozens of picketers instead of thousands would set us up for laughter and dismissal. Lawsuits were mentioned that will cost thousands of dollars, and while that might work for the wealthy, for us it is wasting money better invested in our cultural community. These tactics worked for other groups because the other groups did something we have yet to do. Want to move beyond organized crime or organized buffoonery? Try organizing our culture!

In the Italian immigrants' efforts to become American they es-
chewed education in favor of work; and only later, on the shoulders
of money, began to consider the benefits of formal education. We
were above the average in income long before we were above the average in education. When we sent our children to school, we thought
we were doing the right thing, and so we focused on getting scholarships, money that however well intended, would take our children
further away from their Italian-American neighborhoods and families where ethnic identities were formed and maintained. We re-
belled against earlier generations, who didn't trust education, who
had a natural sense of the changes that would occur in school, and
feared what they didn't know. The basis of fear is ignorance—exactly
what we are facing today.

Those of us born and raised in Little Italys who went to school,
left our homes with a memory and a sense of being Italian American
that was reinforced in those neighborhoods. Without transmitting
that memory to the next generation we lost them. The more education they receive, the further they get from us, and the protection
those communities offered. The result is the creation of Americans
with Italian names who do not see anything wrong in writing, pro-
ducing, directing, and acting in films that, while protected by the
First Amendment, offend other Italian Americans. So where's the
disconnect? To get our culture back, we need to learn from Black
America.

Let's take a brief look at African-American history. When white
people watched African slaves entertaining themselves on planta-
tions, they imitated them through minstrel shows that quickly became popular throughout the country. When freed slaves wanted to
make their way into mainstream U.S. entertainment, they were limited to playing in those same minstrel shows. They outdid the white
actors and in the process brought a little more humanity to their portrayals. As soon as a Black middle class evolved, Blacks took offense
at these portrayals and protested in much the same way the Italian-

American community has for over 80 years. But they didn't limit their strategies to protest. Led by such intellectuals as Harvard educated W.E.B. DuBois, they focused on developing what he referred to as the "Talented Tenth." Through the establishment of Black colleges, Black studies, Black businesses, Black cultural products and consumers, African Americans educated themselves and by the 1920s created arts to be studied and emulated; by the 1960s they created a social and political awareness that challenged racist histories and legacies, and by the 1970s were able to produce independent filmmakers such as Spike Lee and television producers like Bill Cosby who made sure the rest of the world saw their lives in different ways.

While Italian Americans have been busy becoming good Americans, America has spent a great deal of time nurturing what we might call our "Untalented Tenth." Why has the bottom of Italian-American culture gained the spotlight and infamy? Because we have never organized our culture the way others have, and now we are paying for it by fighting sophisticated image-makers with out-of-date weapons.

Basta with using neighborhood strategies to attack national problems. You can't think locally and act globally. We must nationalize the education of Italian Americans first, in order to understand why the Coppolas, Scorseses, Chases achieved success through the minstrel-show mill and, furthermore, why not a single Italian American with any kind of real power in politics, the media, the arts, or religion ever came to the aid of those who wanted to protest defamation of Italian Americans. Second, you need to understand why you don't know, but should know, names like Ardizzone, Bacarella, Ciabattari, deVries, Ermelino, Farella, Gillan, Hendin, Ingrasciotta, Krase, Lentricchia, Musolino, Norelli, Postiglione, Rimanelli, Savoca, Timpanelli, Valerio, and Zandy.

If you believe that *Jersey Shore* on MTV is really gangsters without guns, then you should do something about it. But since when have we become afraid of our youth? Since when has the public behavior of seven 20-something kids been something to pay attention to? This shows that kids don't really know what it means to be Italian American outside of their family; it also shows that we probably don't know our kids as well as we think we do. And if we don't get to know them, there will be no one (or the very few) who will follow us in perpetuating the various national organizations.

What MTV produces is legally their right. Had we done our work right over the past eighty years, others would have joined us in confronting defamatory programs. Had we educated our children, we might not have created those MTV employees who produce and maintain this show. So don't blame MTV; we have failed ourselves.

When you don't see your reflection in a mirror you begin to look for other identities to take on; you become the figurative vampire, living off the blood of others; and that's just what these *Jersey Shore* kids are doing. We know they are no more Italian than the pizzas of Pizza Hut or the food of Olive Garden, so why the protests? Because, as some of the leaders have said, this is the way the rest of the country sees us as? Really? Want to know this for a statistical fact? Commission a serious study to check on it! Contact the Italian-American communities throughout the U.S. and begin communicating, sharing ideas, strategies and resources.

Want to change *Jersey Shore*? Give The Situation and all his buddies scholarships to study in Italy. Let them go to the Mediterranean shore and see if they can entertain audiences acting like that.

To kill an infestation, you can target every instance and keep busy stamping it out one bug at a time, or you can locate the source. I suggest we form a multi-fronted strategy that focuses on the nest.

We may think we have created Italian America, but we have yet to create Italian Americans.

2. Interviews

Italian Americans in the Trap of Television
Interview with Maria Laurino·

Italian Americans need to end their obsession with their image in the television media. Television, in general, tends to caricature reality; it likes showing things that are over the top. This is not about Italian Americans—it is about the media; it's about reality television.

The controversy over MTV's Jersey Shore and the Calandra Institute's colloquium on the guido lifestyle should not be resolved by censorship. It is only through dialogue that you are going to better understand these complex issues of ethnic identity and the media, and further the discussion. Censoring dialogue is always a dangerous act. It reveals a kind of ethnic nationalism that is only about pride and doesn't allow for any kind of questioning or dissent.

What do you think of the way ethnicity—and Italian Americans in particular—are portrayed on American television?

I haven't seen this particular MTV show but from what I have read it reminds me of other sitcoms and reality shows with Italian-American characters. One of the problems in portraying ethnicity on television is that television, in general, tends to caricature reality; it likes showing things that are over the top. The media, and especially television, tends to see everything in broad strokes. Television—and especially reality TV shows—are not interested in nuances as a novelist or an essayist would be. The reason is simple: the media has its own agenda, it has to get the ratings up, it has to make money; they are more concerned about the marketplace than about the issues. And one of the difficulties in portraying ethnic groups is that all these groups have been here for a long time, and when you get, for instance, to the fifth generation of Italian Americans, it is so much harder to get at the nuances of their identity. In the past ten years or so, I think American culture has become cruder and less interested in nuances, and so the portrayal has become even less sophisticated. Just as more and more Italian Americans become as-

· By Ottorino Cappelli

similated, their ethnic identity is portrayed in a way that actually reflects a very small group of people...but nobody is really interested in a more nuanced work.

Some in the Italian American community think that such misrepresentation of ethnic identity in the media is something that regards Italian Americans more than other groups. We often hear that a show like Jersey Shore *would have never been mad about Jews or African-Americans.*

I don't think so. A couple of months ago, I went to a talk to present my newest book in Staten Island and there were many questions about this. "Why do they portray us this way?" people would ask. I responded that this is not about Italian Americans—it is about the media; it's about reality television. If you read newspaper accounts of the making of reality shows, you see how participants are denied sleep, offered lots of alcohol—all to get them to do something outrageous. And people are ready and willing to do this just to get on television. There was nothing "ethnic" about the "Balloon Boy" spectacle. Ethnic groups will always be appealing to broadcasters because they can fall back on certain images and stereotypes. I think that the media would do anything to improve their ratings to earn money, so they push the boundaries of taste. And it seems that the American people are responding, and even fighting for their 15 minutes of fame. In that way, I think the culture has shifted a lot in the past few decades.

Talking about the guido phenomenon, its roots can be traced to the character of Tony Manero, played by John Travolta in Saturday Night Fever. *So, again, we have an interesting interplay between Italian-American reality and its representation.*

There is something fascinating about the relationship between Italian American identity and the image of Tony Manero. When I was researching my book *Were You Always an Italian?* I came across an article by Nick Cohen, a British journalist who wrote the feature story about young people from Bensonhurst in *New York Magazine* that the film *Saturday Night Fever* was based on. Years later he published a confession in *New York Magazine* that the feature story he wrote was made up. This was supposed to be a piece of journalism about Italian Americans in Bensonhurst. He wrote that his editors wanted a certain image of Italian Americans and he went and spent some time in Bensonhurst, but he realized he could not really figure out who they were. He found that he could not make inroads into a culture he was not part of. So, based on what he saw, he created Tony Manero out of his imagination. What fascinates me is indeed that Tony Manero is the fictional creation of an English journalist born in Northern Ireland. What is this telling us about ethnic identity? How real is it and to what extent do we just imitate what we see in films? It's really hard to figure out because it's a bit of a chicken-and-egg question: who came first, the guidos or the guido portrayal that someone then decided to imitate? John Travolta was such an appealing character, an amazing dancer, a handsome man in an enormously popular movie. So many kids must have thought, "Hey, I am from Bensonhurst, I can form some sort of ethnic pride out of that— I'll act like him." They bought into that fictional creation.

You are talking about questions that do not seem to allow for easy answers, including how Italian-American identity is constructed, perceived, and modified. May I assume you must be in favor of scholars and experts investigating these issues?

Of course. And I am very interested in this symposium at the Calandra Institute. All these issues of otherness, of identity, of course push some buttons and touch upon things that might be unpleasant. But it is very dangerous to react by not talking about them. It is only through dialogue that you are going to better understand these complex issues of ethnic identity and further the discussion. Censoring dialogue is always a dangerous act.

Why do you think this censoring attitude is so widespread among ethnic leaders in America, not just among Italian Americans? It seems that the immediate reaction to any disturbing issue is censorship. In this case we go from attempts to stop MTV from "defaming" Italian Americans to an invitation to boycott an academic colloquium about the guido lifestyle.

I think this is a phenomenon that you can see all over the world. It's the result of a sort of fervent nationalism. This kind of ethnic nationalism is only about pride and doesn't allow for any kind of questioning or dissent. Look at the case of Ohran Pamuk, the first Turkish writer to receive the Noble Prize for Literature. A few years ago, he was brought to court for having "offended the Turkish identity" by stating to a Swiss journalist that you can't talk about the genocide of Armenians in Turkey under the Ottoman Empire. Of course we don't have trials against dissidents here in the U.S., but I think the root of the problem is the same: the notion that national pride, or in this case ethnic pride, should never be challenged.

Is there anything that can be done about these issues?

Surely not by watching television reality shows! I think Italian Americans need to put an end to their obsession with their image in the television media. Everything in the media is going to be crude and there is no way you can change this, especially if you start from the wrong assumption—that this is something that only regards Italian Americans. I understand the frustration of the people who are offended by this—I am offended by these portrayals—but this is what American pop culture is becoming. If they really want to think about nuanced images of their own ethnicity—including sometimes controversial images—they should buy and read books by writers from all ethnic groups who are similarly struggling with these issues. And this includes Italian-American writers. Instead of trying to correct the media by censoring them, we should work towards giving these books and ideas much more widespread circulation.

Guido: A Generational Rebellion
Interview with Donna M. Chirico·

I am not sure why mimicking the guido style is any better or worse than folks in a previous generation trying to be like James Dean or pre-Godfather Marlon Brando. It is one generation's rebellion against the previous generation. And it was the disobedience and unruly behavior, now forgotten, that helped to make Sinatra an icon for a particular generation.

This rebellion is needed to move toward establishment of identity as a new group that is independent from the previous generation.

It is outrageous that anyone should claim a specific topic is forbidden ground for interchange. It is in the reasoned discussions about such topics as guido culture that can help us, as a community, reach a consensus.

What do you think of the MTV show Jersey Shore? Is the show as much a depiction of Italian Americans in general as it is of the guidos themselves?

Given the endless stereotypes depicted on television, it is hard to understand why one particular negative portrayal garners criticism while others go unscathed. The irony with *Jersey Shore* is that the controversy within the Italian American community has added to the popularity of the show. Yet, *Jersey Shore* is mild when compared to other shows with respect to language and overt negative behavior. *Cops*, the first reality television show that aired in 1989, with its graphic accounts of hate, violence, and abuse presents highly disturbing imagery that is not tempered by the intervention of actors or any need for figuring out what is real. The show has no narration; the camera just follows the police officers as the crimes or accidents unfold. *Jersey Shore* is a trifle—comic, not brutal in the same direct way.

I am more offended by the gender stereotypes on *Jersey Shore* than by the ethnic ones as these are more insidious. Reality shows continue to send the message that men and women have gender specific behaviors and roles. *Bad Girls Club, The Swan, Married by America*, all offer atrocious depictions of women, their intellects,

· By Ottorino Cappelli

and their ambitions. Watching these shows leads one to assume that every American woman wants to be surgically reconstructed so she can land a rich, hunky guy and live an indolent life poolside while sipping piña coladas. *Jersey Shore* now adds a specific ethnicity to this mix. My sense is that guido/guidette is another version of the gender split that nonetheless supports distinctively American prejudices about men and women. The male characters on *Jersey Shore* use the same epithets about women that other shows use. Women are the generic bitches, sluts, whores, or worse. Listen to how this languaging has made its way into adolescent culture. You will hear 10-year-old girls refer to each other in these terms. Being called a guidette seems innocuous.

College Hill on BET, which presented the first Black reality show with its own set of ethnic stereotypes, shares similar party images with *Jersey Shore*. Perhaps being set on a college campus rather than on a beach offsets the negativity.

As a psychologist, what is your take on this guido culture/style and its relation to the Italian American experience in the New York/New Jersey area?

I am not sure why mimicking the guido style is any better or worse than folks in a previous generation trying to be like James Dean or pre-Godfather Marlon Brando. It is one generation's rebellion against the previous generation. This rebellion is needed to move toward establishment of identity as a new group that is independent from the previous generation. (It is also different from the establishment of individual identity.) Frank Sinatra engaged in despicable personal behaviors, especially toward women, through much of his early life. Somehow these behaviors are blotted out and instead certain Italian Americans canonize the singer as a model Italian American success. Imagine if we had video images of these behaviors. It was the disobedience and unruly behavior, now forgotten, that helped to make Sinatra an icon for a particular generation.

Again, the current guido culture is taking the prevailing traits out there and applying them to a specific ethnic group. It makes sense for a group that is so far removed from its original ethnic identity, as is the case for third, fourth and now fifth generation Italian Americans, that any attempts to recoup that primary sense of ethnicity would now include aspects common to all in a particular age range. The concept that assimilation precludes maintaining ethnic ties is out of date; but the original culture is so distant that what is seen among younger members of a group are the stereotypes, caricatures, or idealized images of that culture that have been handed down along with a cherished family recipe or photograph.

How much of what a 20-year-old knows about Italian culture comes from authentic experience and how much comes from watching films like *The Godfather?* And, what is more disturbing: Nicole (Snooki) of *Jersey Shore* saying "What's up, bitch?" or Carlo in *The Godfather* beating his pregnant wife Connie because she is acting like a bitch? Both images are similar and need to be scrutinized.

Finally, what is your opinion of "anti-defamation" with reference to both this particular episode—including criticism of the Calandra Institute's colloquium on guido culture—and, in general, as an "identity mobilization" tool?

I am a scholar. The word itself comes to us from the Greek via Latin for school. The implication is that a school is a place where lectures are given, where conversations and philosophies are discussed and debated. It is outrageous that anyone should claim a specific topic is forbidden ground for interchange. Conversations about *Jersey Shore, Cops, College Hill* and similar shows are taking place in classrooms throughout the United States. It is essential that young people discuss what they are seeing so they can process these ideas and images in rational way. The Calandra Institute as the leading center of research on Italian American concerns is obliged to take the lead on this issue and present the controversy in a scholarly way open to debate by all.

Identity formation is a central component in the movement toward maturity and psychological health. Young people must role play. They must explore identities to find identity. In the arena of social psychology, multicultural theory argues that having a strong in-group identification, and by implication a secure sense of ethnic identity, allows the individual to display greater tolerance for the out-group. In this model, having a strong Italian American identity allows a person to explore alternative ways to assimilate or achieve from those particular to Italian American culture because these would not be seen as repellant or being at odds with Italian American culture per se. One can then accept being Italian American as part of a personal identity that includes other dimensions as opposed to claiming to be solely Italian American on the basis of what the in-group deems acceptable. This individual is able to live outside the "old neighborhood" and not feel that doing so threatens personal identity; one can be Italian American and be part of mainstream society simultaneously.

This ability requires a confidence of personal identity that must be achieved during adolescence through early young adulthood to further identity development through adulthood. In American society at large, it is exceedingly difficult to keep young people away from cultural influences that caregivers may deem inappropriate or detrimental.

My observation is that just as the adolescent must first come to terms with personal identity before moving through adulthood, the Italian American community must establish a sense of group identity before it can have a fully embodied voice in American culture at large that goes beyond the frivolous. I do not assume that there will be solidarity in this identity; yet, there must be a concordat on matters of mutual interest. It is in the reasoned discussions about such topics as guido culture that can help us, as a community, reach a consensus.

Italian Americans between Guidos and Columbus
Interview with Nancy Carnevale·

There is nothing new in certain segments of the community trying to impose their views of what it means to be Italian American on others. This controversy reminds me of recent tensions around the celebration of Columbus Day. On the one hand, identifying with the discoverer of their adopted land was an ideal strategy to gain full inclusion into mainstream America. But on the other hand, in today's era of multiculturalism with a rhetoric that celebrates cultural diversity, the "discovery" of America by Columbus is equated with the beginnings of the demise of native peoples and their cultures. And there are already many Italian Americans who do not celebrate Columbus Day because of what Columbus has come to represent.

It seems to me that this desire to squelch any consideration of the so-called guido culture is a similar attempt by some to impose a uniform identity on a diverse group.

I would like first to ask your opinion, as an Italian American and as an academic, about this discussion born out of the MTV show Jersey Shore— *the existence of a guido youth culture and the legitimacy of intellectual investigation of this phenomenon.*

As an Italian American, I can attest that the guido culture—a northeastern, urban, working-class/lower middle-class youth style— does exist, although the degree to which it coincides with the representations of that culture in the media is a separate question. As an academic, I am always in favor of open discussion and examination of the issues, whatever they may be. To avoid doing so in this case is to perpetuate the myth that there is a right way and a wrong way to be Italian American when, of course, there are many ways; we are a diverse group in terms of generation, lifestyle, politics, etc. I do understand why some Italian Americans feel defamed by certain characterizations in the media. The stereotype of Italian Americans as unsophisticated and lacking in intelligence goes way back. In the early years of Italian migration, children who fell asleep in school be-

· By Ottorino Cappelli

cause they had to stay up late at night helping their mothers finish garments or make artificial flowers so that their families could survive were labeled intellectually inferior. American schools steered them into "steamer classes" for slow learners. Other factors went into this characterization of Italian Americans as unintelligent, but that label stuck and it has been damaging. But to try and suppress exploration of a segment within your ethnic group because it does not conform to your self-image and the public face you want your ethnic group to present, I can't condone that.

This is not the first time that the prominenti *have tried to shape the public image of the Italian-American community in ways that do not entirely reflect the views of people from different classes, generations, etc. As a historian, would you give us some examples?*

These conflicting understandings of ethnic identity among different segments of the Italian American community that we are seeing now remind me of recent tensions around the celebration of Columbus Day. Columbus Day became a federal holiday in 1934. Some Italian Americans had long been advocating for that and with good reason. For years, Italian Americans were a marginalized group. Identifying with the acknowledged discoverer of their adopted land was an ideal strategy to gain full inclusion into mainstream America. But in today's era of multiculturalism with a rhetoric that celebrates cultural diversity, the "discovery" of America by Columbus is equated with the beginning of the demise of native peoples and their cultures. Although Columbus was not unique in his attitudes or actions, he has come to embody the destruction left in the wake of Western expansion. It is hard to see how Italian American children growing up today who are taught this more critical historical view will be able to express their ethnicity through Columbus Day festivities. There are already many Italian Americans who do not celebrate Columbus Day because of what Columbus has come to represent. I understand why many in the Italian American community have trouble hearing alternative opinions on Columbus Day. Traditions are important to Italian Americans and many remember a time when they felt excluded. Columbus Day has been an important public expression of ethnic pride for many years. But like all ethnic traditions, it is an invented one; another one can take its place, one that would not impose a particular vision of *italianità* on the community. It seems to me that this desire to squelch any consideration of the guido subculture is a similar attempt by some to impose a uniform identity on a diverse group.

In your latest book A New Language, A New World: Italian Immigrants in the United States, 1890-1945 *you dug into this subject by focusing specifically on efforts to maintain the language.*

In New York City beginning in the 1920s, leading members of the Italian American community, including educators such as Leonard Covello, began advocating for Italian to be offered in junior high and high schools. Covello and others felt that teaching Italian to the children of Italian immigrants would help raise their self-esteem, which suffered in this era of blatant prejudice against Italian Americans. Essentially, their aim was to create a pan-Italian-American identity, which was, in reality, a fiction since few of these children would have heard standard Italian spoken in their homes and their parents most likely identified with their regions of origin or their *paese*, not with the Italian nation itself. Rather than help Italian American kids take pride in their local origins, including their dialects, Italian American leaders sought to impose their own views of what it meant to be Italian, i.e., to speak standard Italian rather than dialect, to revere Italian high culture, etc. While not all of the *prominenti* disparaged local identities (Covello was respectful of them), many other leading figures did. So there is nothing new in certain segments of the community trying to impose their views of what it means to be Italian American on others, nor is this phenomenon limited to Italian Americans.

Dirty Laundry and Deep Rugs
Interview with Gianfranco Norelli·

The director of Pane Amaro *[Bitter Bread], an acclaimed documentary about the life and history of early Italian immigrants in the U.S., talks about whether sweeping dirt under the rug is the way to deal with undesirable facts. His film touched upon several difficult topics, including the lynching of 39 Italian immigrants across the United States between 1886 and 1916.*

"Occasionally you do find some people who when faced with difficult, uneasy subjects react by closing their eyes; they prefer not to know about them and even try to prevent you from talking about them. They use a metaphor, you know, they say that we shouldn't 'air our dirty laundry in public.' And I think it doesn't advance the conversation. I do believe that we need to explore difficult issues such as this."

There has been a wave of protests lately from the Italian-American community about MTV's reality show Jersey Shore. *Recently, though, some people have harshly criticized the Calandra Institute, a research institution at CUNY, for sponsoring an academic colloquium on the guido lifestyle. What is your opinion on these issues?*

I only saw a few excerpts of *Jersey Shore* and it did not appeal to me. I can see why some people consider it demeaning and offensive. But I think it is important to keep our focus on the fact that if there is a phenomenon among the Italian American youth that is similar to what is portrayed in the show, we need to study it, and we need to understand what causes it and what the consequences are. Only if we understand it can we prevent these stereotypes from becoming common currency in the media.

So I think the Calandra Institute is doing a very important job in sponsoring an academic discussion of this subject—this segment of Italian American youth culture, not just the MTV show. In any group there can be some problematic experiences, but they don't go away just by not talking about them. In a sense, I think we have the responsibility to appropriate these kinds of investigations and dis-

---

· By Ottorino Cappelli

cussions—it is our business, as Italian Americans, more than anybody else's. And there could be no better place than the Calandra Institute, and a colloquium with a social scientist who has studied this phenomenon for a number of years.

In other words, it is one thing if the media exploits a social phenomenon for commercial reasons, and maybe circulates offensive stereotypes, but it is a different matter when a cultural institution addresses the same phenomenon with the purpose of investigating it.

Yes. By trying to understand the roots of what we perceive as a problematic behavior of some Italian American youths, we are not endorsing it in any way, and surely we are not glorifying it. These phenomena may be more or less widespread or isolated, representative or unique, but once we get to the point we are at, we cannot deny that they do exist. And if they exist, it is only by bringing them into full light and by exposing them to serious intellectual scrutiny that we can really understand them. And because we are talking about youths, this is also the only way we can provide young people with the tools to understand whether there is any value for them in this phenomenon, whether there is any good in being associated with it, or whether it may only have negative consequences.

You have had a somewhat similar experience with Pane Amaro. *Your film has also been accused by some people of touching upon subjects that "make us look bad," of talking about things that should not be talked about.*

We have shown *Pane Amaro* in a lot of places, in New York, in Washington, in New Jersey. Lately we showed it in twelve different venues in California, in Nevada, and in Canada. And occasionally, yes, we did have some people lamenting the fact that some scenes should not have been shown. For instance, we talk about things like the lynching of early Italian immigrants a century or so ago. All in all, 39 Italians were lynched across the United States. And some viewers were very disturbed and said we shouldn't be talking about this. It was offending them maybe because it was too graphic, too traumatic—a kind of dark page in our history that some don't want to remember. The majority of viewers, however, found that learning about these episodes that were unknown to them was important and they found it very valuable. But occasionally you do find some people who, when faced with difficult, uneasy subjects react by closing their eyes; they prefer not to know about them and even try to prevent you from talking about them. They use a metaphor, you know, they say that we shouldn't "air our dirty laundry in public." And I think it doesn't advance the conversation.

It is also important to emphasize that such an attitude of denial is not necessarily the typical reaction of all Italian American associations. Your film, for instance, has been supported by the National Italian American Foundation.

Sure. NIAF was one of the most important sources of funding for *Pane Amaro*. They understand the value of serious investigation into our history.

You have deeply investigated the grandfathers and great-grandfathers of today's Italian American youth. Do you think that a subject such as the guido lifestyle would make an interesting topic for one of your next documentaries?

Well, yes. First of all, of course, I'd like to know more about it. And this is why I value any serious investigation on this subject. Documentaries can be a useful way to study an issue and to have it come alive for an audience. And I do believe that we need to explore difficult issues such as this. Sweeping it under the rug will not make it go away.

The View from Italy
Interview with Aldo Grasso·

Journalist, television critic, professor of radio and television history at Catholic University in Milan, Aldo Grasso moderates a forum entitled Television *on* Corriere della Sera's *website where he has established a direct line of communication between readers and television programs.*

We met him in New York and talked at length about controversial programs such as Jersey Shore *and* The Sopranos, *discussed both American and Italian television, and reflected on the media's influence and what happens when politics seeks to influence the media.*

"I was immediately struck by *The Sopranos.* I found the first season fascinating. Not just its content, but its production, how it was made. I later learned that the more traditional Italian-American organizations had started to protest it. But the most surprising thing for me was seeing Italians ride this wave. I remember when Gianfranco Fini, then secretary of the Alleanza Nazionale party, came to America and participated in the protests condemning the stereotypes."

And so Aldo Grasso began a direct debate with Fini in the pages of *Corriere della Sera.* "Before taking these positions, wouldn't it be better to learn more about the issue that we're discussing?" Grasso wrote, suggesting that Fini had never watched an episode of *The Sopranos.* Had he seen it, "given his intelligence and sensitivity, he certainly would not have protested it."

The story continued, and the series became ever more successful while the controversy surrounding it grew. "But it was a backward argument. A mobster who goes to a psychiatrist cannot be seen as stereotypical mobster."

When Grasso came across *Jersey Shore* on MTV and the reactions of the same Italian/American organizations, he thought, "Here we go again. It's the same story repeating itself. They're not watching

---

· By Letizia Airos

89

the programs, they're not discussing the content, but they do have an overarching fear of stereotypes."

In one of your articles you described Jersey Shore *as entertaining and educational. What did you mean by that?*

The two things are connected. In this case the combination is very important because you watch a program when it's entertaining and this, in turn, opens up new worlds that you aren't familiar with. The guido phenomenon was completely new to me; I knew nothing about it. It was an extraordinary discovery to see that there is a way of relating to *italianità* that is no longer a stereotype but, if anything, has become a topos, a standard representation. There are young, second- and third-generation Italian Americans who live like this, who use lots of hair gel, who act in a certain way, who speak in a certain way. They are the children of *Saturday Night Fever* and *Grease*. A new world opened up to me and I entered into it. It was interesting, first of all, from the perspective of representation. You could understand from the way they spoke and expressed themselves how others viewed them.

American television series have always been very successful in Italy, and they have always shown the American world, but up to now they were full of young, cute blonde girls. In this case, a slice of *Italian* America was now on display. For this reason I found it instructive: it allowed us to discover something new in an entertaining way. I think that's what deserves the most attention. I do not find it offensive to anyone.

In the history of Italian television has a particular program ever generated such strong "political" reactions?

Recently there have been these types of political reactions to television programs. Prime Minister Berlusconi has long complained that Italian television dramas focus too narrowly on the Mafia. But we should also realize that Italian dramas about the Mafia are the only ones that sell abroad. Italian TV usually gets to the border of Chiasso [*near Italy's northern border with Switzerland, Eds.*] and stops there. The *Piovra* mini-series was one of the few successful television series abroad.

What kind of television programs do the critics suggest instead?

It's always a maudlin portrait of everything Italian! Berlusconi invokes an Italy that is positive, hard-working, and creative but from a dramatic point of view it's ridiculous. It doesn't hold up. Over the past 10, 15 years, Italian television has relied on one type of bio-graphical drama that airs in two episodes, which is almost always a hagiography. So it's the "lives of saints"—and they are always politicians, athletes and sport stars, real saints, captains of industry, etc.

One particularly good program that aired recently was *Romanzo Criminale* [*Crime Novel*], a series about the famous Magliana gang, the criminal political machine that ruled Rome in the 1970s. It was a fine production, but from the point of view of the image present-ed, it's really embarrassing. What emerges is a portrait of Italian in-stitutions that's mortifying.

So here's the eternal problem: what's valid from a dramatic point of view can cause problems from a political point of view. If we care about social image, then the embarrassment of institutions is understandable. But if we begin to analyze the process, which do we choose? Something interesting from a dramatic point of view or something rewarding from an institutional point of view? When you choose the latter, it's often one-dimensional and boring.

The charges of defamation that some Italian/American organizations have hurled at The Sopranos *and* Jersey Shore *thus are comparable to those of Berlusconi, who thinks that Italian dramas about the Mafia dam-age Italy's image abroad. We are faced with an unwavering attitude that is so-called "patriotic-nationalistic." Politics then dictate the rules of drama, art, etc.*

Yes, the pretense is that politics determines the outcome; rather than making an effort and attempting to dissect and understand a symbolic device, politicians stop short and focus on the most mundane and obvious images.

What politicians in Italy have never understood, with respect to television, is that everything revolves around the "construction of identity." It's not what's said directly on television that has a strong social impact. What matters most is what's said in an indirect way. Television has been instrumental in the construction of a national Italian identity, but that hasn't happened by broadcasting a prime minister's speech or political talk shows.

Let me give you an example. The process of acquiring fluency and literacy in standard Italian and the role that television has played in that process has been plagued with misunderstandings for years. Up to now, credit has always been given to Maestro Manzi's shows which were directed at people who were not literate, saying that "it's never too late to learn" and telling them to watch this or that series. The reality is that the country learned to speak standard Italian through many other successful shows such as *Lascia o Raddoppia* [Double or Nothing, *a quiz show*, Eds.], perhaps the only program with a genuine cult following at the time.

Similarly, political debates rarely affect viewers' choices. There are programs that do not focus squarely on politics but deal with politics in a different way, and they are much more effective. For example, there are afternoon shows for young people, and several in the morning. They convey an idea, a certain ideology, without ever declaring it overtly.

We are therefore faced with a complex problem from a symbolic point of view. If you only look at the most obvious content—how Italians are portrayed, for example—you make huge mistake. We need to look at the "code of communication," understand how a series is structured and grasp its linguistic complexity. It's only by doing this kind of analysis can we understand the different types of representation and ultimately say something more meaningful. But politics rarely takes this next step.

And Romanzo Criminale [Crime Novel], which you mentioned earlier, conveys its own negative message.

If we were to erase all of the anti-heroes from the history of literature, theater, film, there would be very few characters left. From a dramatic point of view, the anti-hero is always far more interesting than the hero. We must acknowledge that there may be anti-heroes simply because it's a fact. There is an interesting question that we, of course, must ask: what justifies the presence of an anti-hero in a story? The reason can be found in an aesthetic point of view. The only ethical question that applies to art is, "Is it done well?" "Is it linguistically compelling and complex?"

Let's go back to The Sopranos *and the type of mobster portrayed in that series as compared with Coppola's* The Godfather. *The television series seems to destroy the image, the myth. It makes him insecure, weak. A gangster has never been depicted in this way.*

From a narrative perspective, *The Sopranos* is one of the best American television series produced in recent memory. Even if we looked beyond the Italian/American element, it would still be a very interesting series. The genius of *The Sopranos* lies in its ability to simultaneously show us the Mafia while depicting other aspects that we would have never considered before.

There are still the typical Mafia stereotypes, including heinous criminal acts, but at the same time it's as if Tony Soprano's therapy sessions do not belong to him alone, but to the whole phenomenon. What comes out expresses his vulnerability, and the family's role is completely different from how a Mafia family was depicted before. It's a middle-class family with its own problems, especially raising children who turn against their parents. There's an incredible level of complexity. The Mafia becomes a pretext and has nothing to do with old stereotypes. The interesting aspect in this story is the portrayal of this vulnerability and everything else that goes against the Mafia's usual iconography, including the characters' insecurities: they are the real victims!

It's still a story set in an area controlled by the Mafia. But I find nothing offensive about it. It seems to me that destroying the traditional image of the Mafia from within has been an enormous service to Italy and to Italian Americans.

Getting back to Jersey Shore, *from a sociological point of view, and not from the standpoint of media studies, you compared the cast to similar Italian characters,* i tammarri *[the idiots]. These types of young people exist all over Italy, not just in New Jersey.*

I find this very interesting. Usually when *i tamarri* [the idiots] are depicted in Italian movies or on television, they become caricatures. They are never shown for who they really are—unless it's a good documentary, but that's extremely rare. What happens on *Jersey Shore* is significant. These aren't caricatures but far more realistic and captivating photographic portraits. I think that a caricature might be offensive, but a realistic representation can't be. This understanding brings a level of depth that allows me to fill in the gaps in some way. If I see an accident on the street, I find myself faced with a very dramatic moment, but it's not that I think that life is all drama.

I think that reality shows are interesting, even in the case of *Grande Fratello* [*Big Brother*] when we're in the 10th or 11th season, and frankly, it becomes annoying. But there are times when those young people's defenses are completely down and they don't even notice the television cameras. What emerges is a portrait of a certain group of young people that is much more interesting than what is often scripted. So the value of *Jersey Shore* is wrapped up in the genre of reality show. The television cameras were turned on and they showed us a certain reality that no writer would have been able to script.

But many people say that the cast was pushed to exaggerate.

The general claim is that there's a tendency to play up some things because the cameras are rolling and the cast knows it. But we must try to understand the image while keeping the frame in mind. We must assess what we're seeing in terms of this framework. It's not a documentary, it's not investigative journalism. We should not confuse the two—it's a reality show.

This is a question for you more as a parent than as a scholar. Don't we have to worry about our kids who might see this show as a model, as an ideal way of life?

The discussion here is more complex. Studies on the effects of media have shown that there is no cause and effect relationship in a direct way. It's as if television were a family member, a guest who talks about some things. The relationship is there, but it's indirect. It's also not true that kids watch that much television. They do so in a casual, and, again, indirect way, like the Internet. So they won't watch an entire episode, but only the parts they choose to see. Finally, to determine the impact of television it's important to consider the mediation of the family, which plays a key role. Let me give you another example. Many studies have indeed shown the negative influence of television, especially on children who were left alone in front of the TV set for several hours, often in low-income families where parents used the television as a kind of babysitter while they were at work. It was also found that there were no books, no newspapers in those homes. In short, where the mediation of the family is irrelevant, television's effects are felt more profoundly. But as the family structure becomes more complex, and mediation becomes more pronounced, those effects are reduced. So the problem is not so much television, but the family structure. If we bring the discussion back to *Grande Fratello* [*Big Brother*], we see that these models take hold where there are few defenses. Where there's a strong family structure, where people talk and discuss, the effect is minimal and very often it's actually experienced in an ironic way.

We should also discuss the issue of political control over television programming. We see this in both Italy and America when groups want to protest certain depictions which they have deemed harmful or defamatory.

In Italy, the real detrimental effect, not only by Berlusconi but by all politicians, occurred when RAI television and public service stations were completely taken over. It's a mistake to rely on political officials rather than media professionals when it comes to broadcasting. This determines and hampers the image that television creates and presents. For example, all of the television dramas produced in Italy over the last twenty years have had some political implication. One drama was made to satisfy one political group, another was made for another political group, and so on.

The real trial that Italian television is going through has to do with the excessive influence of politics. And every time politicians become interested in film, television, and theater, they end up acting in a very unrefined, one-sided manner. They have only one goal—to show a positive image. A dramatist's aim is completely different.

As for Italian Americans, I think they carry the rhetoric of Fascism with them. Historically there hasn't been a way for them to absorb and process the change. They understood the stereotype of one national identity, but they have not gone through the process of understanding the next one. Without knowing it, as they fight the stereotypes created by others, they unwittingly become victims of the same stereotyping.

Then I watch RAI International and I want to tear my hair out. Italian/American organizations should fight for RAI International. How is Italy being portrayed? It is RAI that should broadcast programs such as *Jersey Shore* while contextualizing and explaining them, and engaging in interesting and thought-provoking discussions!

Among other things, this could help Italians understand how difficult it is to be "G2," second- and third-generation Italian American.

Definitely. They could really invest in it and add English subtitles to Italian news programs, since many Americans of Italian origin, particularly young people, no longer speak our language. These are obvious opportunities that RAI has missed. They claim that they have little money but the issue is that the budget could be allocated differently. Italian Americans would do better to complain about RAI International instead of how American television represents *italianità*.

3. The Colloquium

Guido: An Italian/American Youth Style
Introductory Remarks
by Anthony Julian Tamburri

This colloquium is not about the MTV show Jersey Shore *and it does not justify it in any manner. This colloquium is about the phenomenon of the guido that, regardless of its merits or lack thereof, has its origins and is associated with Italians in America.*

Whether one likes it or not, this component of Italian/American youth–an articulation of cultural expression, call it what one wishes–does exist.

We are not asking anyone "to accept" this or any other "subculture" that may exist in the Italian/American community. Yet, precisely because this culture has been showcased on television, and precisely because it has remained unknown to many, we need to be sure that we can speak to it in an informed manner....

First, I want to thank those who have helped make this colloquium possible. At the top of the list are Professor Donald Tricarico and Johnny DeCarlo, for accepting our invitation and–in light of the heated discussions that followed our initial press release–for being here today. That said, I cannot underscore enough that fact that they are our guests here at the Calandra Institute, as you all are. We expect that all present, who might disagree with anything said today, will do so in a respectful manner. We here at Calandra will simply not tolerate any gratuitous insults or vituperous offense.

I also want to thank Dr. Joseph Sciorra, who organized this event, and Dr. Fred Gardaphé who found himself in the unenviable position of being the object of unflattering commentary and who responded with much grace and aplomb. Finally, I need to thank *Italics*, under the direction of William Schempp, and i-Italy.org, under the direction of Letizia Airos and Dr. Ottorino Cappelli. These two outlets, both now multimedia, while located in New York, can prove to be the national networks for all things Italians. This, too, we shall explore in the near future.

Now, let me start out by doing what we were taught not to do in Ciceronian Rhetorical Studies and underscore what this is not. Our colloquium is *not* an "educational" lecture, as someone stated to me; in our brief announcement nowhere is this adjective present. It is also *not* geared to "young and impressionable minds," as someone wrote. Though I would submit to all of you present that many undergraduate college courses across the country address social issues much more debatable than the one we shall discuss here today. Our intended audience is a general one, open to the public at large. Also, I need to underscore further that this a colloquium (1) that does *not* glorify the notion of this one component of Italian/American youth about which little is known, and (2) that does *not* glorify the MTV show *Jersey Shore*.

As for the first point, whether one likes it or not, there is this component of Italian/American youth—an articulation of cultural expression, call it what one wishes—that manifests itself in this manner and that has been dubbed guido. We may not like it, but it does exist, as there are also members of other ethnicities that have taken on what is widely considered negative nomenclature and adopted it as their moniker. I would remind the audience of the gangsta rap group that eventually called itself by the abbreviation NWA (Niggers With Attitude), which lasted from 1986-1991. The Afrcan/American community addressed this and other issues they found problematic, and continues to do so today.

We are not asking anyone "to accept" this or any other "subculture" that may exist in the Italian/American community. Yet, precisely because this culture has been showcased on television, and precisely because it has remained unknown to many, we need to be sure that we can speak to it in an informed manner, rather than let a commercial enterprise that is MTV decide to appropriate it, distort it, pass it off as real and authentic, and, hence, representative (falsely, I would add) of Italian/American youth at large. For as much as those in our community who are familiar with this subculture and may not like it, we simply need to be aware of it and, further, know its roots so we can better comprehend its existence in an informed manner.

Like some adults in our community, some of our young engage in lifestyles that are not acceptable to the majority. The question, then, is what do we do about it? As a community at large, and especially our national organizations and institutes, we need to investigate such phenomena in order to be as informed as possible about what is happening beyond the center, the mainstream, of our community.

As for the second point in my opening paragraphs, our colloquium was indeed prompted by the MTV show, the entire process of which raised a series of questions and angered Italian Americans, just as NWA did in the African/American community. But this colloquium is *not* about the show and it does *not* justify it any manner; nowhere did we imply either. This colloquium is about the phenomenon of the guido that, regardless of its merits or lack thereof, has its origins and is associated with Italians in America.

Such problematic questions, as I have discussed many times with others in the past, are what we as a community at large have not addressed. We have, instead, let others take possession of these issues—Italian Americans and non-Italian Americans in the media, for example—and we have been left to react, and we have done so separately. We have rarely, as a community, had our own forums on this and other matters that have arisen in the past once we have gone through that primary phase of reacting to the issue, something valid by all means but only a first step. (I have, for instance, blogged about this in the past with regard to the lack of substantive cultural philanthropy; only one national organization has engaged in endowed professorships and individuals in this regard are far and few in between.)

Whether it is this current issue, or what some have previously dubbed the "Madonna" factor and all the "wannabes" of the 1990s, or the more general issue of why we are often associated with much troubling imagery such as, first and foremost, organized crime, as a community at large we have not taken possession of the discussion. We have not, that is, engaged in any profound discussion and investigation of the "whys" and "what-fors" of any of the hot-button issues mentioned above, or any other matter, as far as I know, that have troubled members of the Italian/American community.

This colloquium is a first step in such a practice. That said, let me also underscore that this colloquium can indeed be a first-step in our (not just Calandra's, but the entire Italian/American community's) investigation of this and other issues that some find problematic.

In order for us to embark on such a path, therefore, I am asking those in leadership positions of NIAF, NOIAW, OSIA, and UNICO here present today to remain after the conclusion of this event so we might share some preliminary ideas on what to do next. Subsequent to this meeting, we can surely discuss what other problematic issues we need to address in a more analytical manner than we have not done before.

This is a long-term commitment that asks us to gather as a community of Italian Americans at large (NIAF, NOIAW, OSIA, UNICO, other national Italian/American organizations such as AATI and AIHA, ILICA, and scholars, teachers, and writers) and investigate the myriad topics such as those mentioned above that others have defined for us. Other ethnicities have done so, as I mentioned above with regard to NWA. I especially have in mind the so-called "town-gown" combination of, for instance, Bill Cosby and Professor Alvin Poussaint. The Italian and Italian/American communities here in the United States have not done so, and I would submit to you that, as much of a stretch as it may seem in this context, the current situation of the Advanced Placement Exam in Italian is symptomatic of such an absence of these practices.[44]

---

[44] At the time of these opening remarks, the College Board has suspended the Advanced

As you well know, the Calandra Institute is a university research institute dedicated to, among other things, the study, research, and analysis of Italian/American history and culture, which includes investigating even, or dare I say equally so, those issues that we find problematic. That said, I am announcing a new program we will soon launch, the occasional meeting of the minds, which will discuss contemporary issues we should indeed be addressing. These meetings will be broadcast live on the Internet by *Italics*, and subsequently archived online in order to be accessible for later viewing.

In closing, I am confident this will prove to be the productively informative event it was originally planned to be.

Placement Program in Italian, and its future was still uncertain. Since then, however, under the leadership of the Italian Embassy in Washington, D.C. and the Council of Presidents of Major Italian American Organizations, the Italian and Italian/American communities in the United States did rally together, and the AP Program in Italian was re-instated.

Guidos on MTV: Tangled Up in the Feedback Loop
by Donald Tricarico

Why has MTV produced a youth culture reality show that showcases guido and Italian identity? Guido offers a symbol that specifically identifies the brand; Italian ethnicity makes the brand more salient. Guido combines a commodified youth party culture with a style that has street culture roots. [...]

Guido is a struggle for recognition and respect by an age fraction that privileges consumption rather than formal education, reflecting class differences in an ethnic culture that continues to evolve in metropolitan New York City and throughout the northeast. [...]

Youth may turn more to ethnicity to authenticate their cool and preserve privileged insider status as in hip-hop. However, this is denied by a vocal anti-defamation position that reduces guido to a category of ethnic prejudice. It is my view that this slights a vernacular Italian American culture that ironically is better defined as a challenge to generalizations and stereotypes that underpin historic ethnic slurs.

Social identities are problematic because they are transacted by individuals and groups with disparate interests and resources. Guido has emerged as a highly contested identity now that it is being transacted in the wider public discourse. The MTV reality show *Jersey Shore* demonstrates the power of the corporate media to shape discourse in the popular culture. Global companies like Nike and MTV "sell cool" to young people. Malcolm Gladwell (1997) has pointed out that marketing strategies "hunt" for trends that are "cool" —styles created by young people like skateboarding and rapping over dance music records. Appropriation for sale to a mass youth market accelerates what Gladwell characterizes as a "feedback loop" that transforms initial statements, which were hardly invented in a pop culture vacuum.

My research interests have centered on Italian American vernacular culture in New York City. The first installment was a doctoral dissertation on the Italian American neighborhood in Greenwich Village where my mother's side of the family settled before 1900 and where I was born and baptized (at St. Anthony's of Padua on Sullivan Street). While the sociological literature framed the ethnic neighborhood as a staging ground for immigrants, community institutions adapted to the city in the second and third generation (Tricarico 1984).

Since the late 1980s I have paid close attention to the relationship between Italian ethnicity and youth popular culture identified with guido. Guido was organically connected to local Italian neighborhood culture especially in the outer boroughs and was likewise an adaptation of ethnicity to the city and the larger culture at a particular historical juncture. Guido is a form of "youth agency," the central concept in the youth studies field referring to the "meaning-making, narratives, cultural productions, and social engagements" of young people in relation to popular culture (Maira and Soep 2004: 246). Youth culture is predicated on structural transformations associated with "late capitalism" that create an age category defined by expressive consumption. Youth culture studies focus on expressive repertoires or styles, especially visual signifiers or a "look," fabricated out of symbolic commodities and media imagery. A small body of research in the United States documents the role of youth agency in the emergence of social and cultural forms that are "hybrids" of ethnicity and American popular culture (Maira 2002; Lipsitz 1990).

Youth styles of leisure in the city's Italian American neighborhoods were historically inhibited by economic scarcity and ethnic traditions. Youth aged-out to adulthood by the end of their teens which partially explains formidable high-school drop-out rates for local Italian Americans into the 1980s. Working-class youth styles were labeled "greaser"—a taste culture that stigmatized the dirty labor of teenagers who worked on automobiles and other machines. The greasy look of lower-class teenagers was assigned to ethnic minorities with ambiguous whiteness, notably Italian Americans with stereotypically dark and "oily" complexions.

Guido signals a departure from greaser in two key respects. First, there were greater opportunities for hedonistic consumption; it is the franchise of immigrant and second Italian generation youth to consume commodified leisure styles that have proliferated in American youth culture since the 1970s. Second, ethnicity was mobilized for consumption that transcended *local* greaser styles. An ethnic claim to cool, or prestigious cultural capital, has been contested from the outset.

A galvanizing event was the disco craze of the 1970s. An early feedback loop was evident when 1977 movie *Saturday Night Fever* portrayed the vernacular disco styles of working-class Italian Americans in southern Brooklyn neighborhoods like Bensonhurst with an Italian ancestry population over 100,000 in 1980. The film, in turn, supplied an origin myth for a critical mass of young people in the city's Italian American neighborhoods that had acquired the leisure and the discretionary income to cultivate a style of consumption based on clubbing.

Popular culture provides "a free space for the imagination—an area liberated from old restraints and repressions, a place where desire did not have to be justified and explained" (Lipsitz 1994: 9). Disco promised a more sweeping social transformation than greaser. The intense sensuality of club culture offered symbolic escape from lower-class status and a negatively privileged ethnicity through the "work" of leisure and the youthful body (Fikentscher 2000). It became the dominant style of the city's Italian American neighborhoods by the 1980s. Italian ethnicity was invoked to establish a franchise on electronic dance music like freestyle and house. An ethnic niche was delineated by Italian American DJs, producers, and club owners that imprinted on the local dance music station WKTU, "The Beat of New York."

While an "underground" club culture aesthetic offers youth an opportunity to "escape class" (Thornton 1995), local Italian American youth consumed mass commercial culture to become American and to escape to a higher class. Moreover, this was in the name of ethnicity, which suggests that they didn't want to become somebody else but become an Italian American who was a somebody. The symbolic work of blending youth style and ethnic identity is possible because "traditional resources" and "inherited meanings" have "lost their legitimacy for a good proportion of young people" (Willis 1990:10). Nevertheless, subcultural ideology has professed commitment to a traditional ethnic culture compartmentalized offstage in family settings. Family culture has been reconciled with style by clubbing with relatives and making ethnic peers cugines.

Identifying youth style with ethnicity was an extension of the way Italian Americans positioned themselves in the city. A style cultivated in local Italian neighborhoods set youth apart when they arrived en masse in the club culture scene. Italian ethnicity drew boundaries with local youth cultures defined by race and class; to that extent, consumption style expressed positioning in status hierarchies in the city and American society. Italian ethnicity managed a relationship with Black and Latino youth who were turf rivals but also formidable influences in dance club culture, making it possible to selectively appropriate their styles without surrendering racial claims. An Italian youth identity was also transacted with club culture elites. While Italian American youth used ethnicity to express cultural difference, the possibility of becoming somebody else was checked by the arbiters of cool in Manhattan clubs like Studio 54 and Limelight. Guido labeled the "bridge and tunnel" style of Italian American; the invasion of "tacky shirtless guidos jumping around pumping their fists" portended the defeat of underground cool at Exit in 2002 (a post on the Clubplanet message board July 11, 2002 and accessed January 22, 2002). The invidious status politics of club culture is involved in naming "gino" in Toronto; the Hamptons nightlife scene has recently gestated a category known as "joey" which is a "bridge and tunnel" designation and a second generation synonym for guido.

Guido emerges as a youth culture identity symbol in transaction inside and across the ethnic boundary. It was interchangeable with the name cugine through the 1980s. *Cugino* is the Italian word for cousin and expresses a fictional kinship within the youth style community as a form of ethnic solidarity. It is plausible that guido may have named the style of "off the boat" Italian males within the ethnic community, reflecting the status politics of the immigrant queue. However, guido emerged in the lexicon of Manhattan club culture elites to disparage an upstart outer borough style (Tricarico 2008). Identifying with guido was a way of talking back to or opposing club culture stigma as well as subsuming invidious distinctions inside the ethnic boundary, and the reversal of ethnic stigma was harvested for the accumulation of youth culture capital. An ethnography of a chat room scene established by and for subcultural youth that I conducted in 2000 and 2001 found the use of historic slurs of guinea and wop alongside guido. Rhetorical strategies manipulated symbols of inferior status and outsiderness into badges of ethnic authenticity that were treated as youth culture capital. At this point, guido becomes a symbolic reversal like "nigga" that distills a quintessential ethnicity and its usage warrants a careful determination of insider status.

Guido is an identity option when certain symbolic repertoires are in evidence—a look, a sound, and an attitude read by those who are literate in local youth culture codes. It is the outcome of a particular youth agency and it is recognized as self-authored; collective agency was asserted in the song "Guido Rap" recorded by a local Italian American DJ circa 1987 and distributed in subcultural venues. It is a "mix and match" style, what the cultural studies approach refers to as a "bricolage" of symbols. Appropriation is unified by ethnicity and meaningful within a local youth style tradition. This accounts for the survival of greaser elements like slicked-backed hair and sleeveless undershirts and themes like masculine aggression which have been increasingly stylized by the all-consuming project of bodily display—"looking ripped" as an outcome of particular leisure routines (the look of a somebody without a typical working-class Italian American body). Stylized masculinity is a check on repertoires associated with femininity and gay fashion trends like sculpted eyebrows and even dancing; the signature "fist pump" dance style is a masculinist street culture gesture.

Identity choices are made in social contexts. The chat room that I studied revealed a marked ambivalence about guido as an identity symbol. While guido was an option for individual and group identity, it was not a successful strategy for attracting youth to a room. A viable scene manipulated Italian ethnicity. Being Italian accommodated a variance in style that transcended symbolic elements and performances specific to guido-like fist-pumping and house music. An inclusive ethnicity also facilitated cyber-networking into the metropolitan diaspora.

On the other hand, ethnicity was submerged by the organization New Jersey Guido established in 2002. A subcultural ideology elaborated on its website "redefined guido" as "youth, beauty, and flash." The new style spectacle was "the crazy ass New Jersey scene" centered on clubs in certain shore towns, not Bensonhurst which lost half of its Italian population between 1980 and 2000, although a line can be drawn connecting the Jersey Shore to southern Brooklyn and then Staten Island which became heavily Italian American (i.e., "Staten Italy") when the Verrazano Bridge opened in the 1960s. (An iconic presence in *Saturday Night Fever*, the bridge was immediately dubbed "the guinea gangplank" by truckers on CB radio.) New Jersey Guido was recently renamed Night Life Society, a "Social Network for Night Life" aspiring to a still more inclusive style. The new site has a forum for Latinos but not Italian Americans. This shift left an opening for MTV which flagrantly markets the ethnic cool of guidos and guidettes on *Jersey Shore*. The casting call posted on the Internet profiled a club "hottie" who is also a "loud and proud Italian." Symbolic identification with Italian ancestry is scripted on the show. There is a nod to a traditional family morality in awkward juxtaposition to the hook-up culture.

Why has MTV produced a youth culture reality show that showcases guido and Italian identity? Guido offers a symbol that specifically identifies the brand; Italian ethnicity makes the brand more salient. Guido combines a commodified youth party culture with a style that has street culture roots—the element of urban authenticity that sells Black youth culture in the suburbs. Guido began selectively poaching hip-hop before it diffused to mainstream youth. MTV exploited a connection to gangsta when it cast guido as "the hottest pimps." As such, guido can appeal to a suburban youth market that crosses over to hip-hop but not Blackness. While *American Bandstand* sanitized greaser in the 1960s, *Jersey Shore* has scripted moral panic with depictions of brawling and licentious sex.

MTV is hardly the first attempt to merchandise guido style. The reality TV show *Growing Up Gotti* portrayed guido style but refrained from using the symbol. A designer menswear company called Guido New York appropriated the identity symbol of a disenfranchised urban youth subculture. In one promotional image, the elevated B train tracks that run along New Utrecht Avenue and 86th Street unmistakably marks the historic guido turf of southern Brooklyn. Other images portray tough posing males in track suits; one is leaning against a cool car while holding a baseball bat—a signifier of street culture, not the sport. Designs reflected a "tough-guy sex appeal" in "marked contrast to the metrosexual ambiguity that has dominated the marketplace in recent years." Mafia masculinity was referenced when one of John Gotti's celebrity grandsons was used as a runway model for the company's 2004 line. However, in marked contrast to FUBU, the advertising campaign distanced itself from the subculture it was merchandising. Guido New York conceded that "the name 'guido'" is an "image" or "stereotype" that "may be perceived as negative," in particular "something that is less desirable" and "less than classy." Its design signature "re-contextualized and appropriated the word not the stereotype."

By flaunting the stereotype MTV may be selling guido as uncool to cool kids everywhere. The producers of the show are probably young and cool enough to be aware that guido is widely ridiculed and vilified on Internet sites like YouTube and Urban Dictionary. (The frequency of Italian surnames in the show's credits suggests another intra-group dynamic.) Reality TV specializes in the depiction of taste cultures that invite the disdain of tasteful constituencies; there happens to be a subgenre just for Italian Americans in *Growing Up Gotti*, *The Real Housewives of New Jersey*, and MTV's *True Life: Staten Island*. Nouveau riche Italian Americans are also typed in the role of conspicuous vulgar consumption in fictional narratives like *The Sopranos* and *Married to the Mob*, reinforcing the connection between tasteless consumption and moral and criminal deviance. There is perhaps a clue in media depictions of arriviste Italian Americans for an interpretation of guido. Conspicuous consumption salves a status wound caused by negatively privileged ethnicity: the collective ethnic memory of poverty, stunted formal education, dirty labor, and worse. Guido is a struggle for recognition and respect that privileges consumption rather than formal education, reflecting class differences in an ethnic group.

Jersey Shore is a particular representation of guido that has the weight of reality because it is constructed in the mass media. Ratings have established its commercial success and promise a return engagement. This has reverberated in the popular culture notably in other prestigious mass media outlets and on the Internet. The ongoing study of guido as youth culture has to take measure of *Jersey Shore's* impact on the feedback loop. Guido has been solidified as a category of the media culture that can be expected to shore up identity performances in the urban style spectacle. In particular, media celebrity may have yielded highly visible style leaders who can figure in commercial endorsements for commodities appropriated by youth themselves like Armani Exchange and Ed Hardy T-shirts. Celebrities can be enlisted to sell signature styles to youth who identify with the brand irrespective of the organic connections of ethnicity, class, and place.

Media recognition can nourish a second-generation youth style outside ethnic neighborhood culture; the Gotti reality TV show energized a guido scene on Long Island. The Internet, in particular, offers new opportunities to network and to stage a wider conversation about subcultural ideology amid a welter of disparaging content. New media venues include the possibility of challenging the MTV brand; this has already occurred on the Night Life Society site, especially on the part of the founder who still regards himself as "more or less the official guido spokesperson." The welter of sites that denigrate guido on the Internet can reinforce subcultural boundaries. Italian American youth may turn more to ethnicity to authenticate their cool and preserve privileged insider status as in hip- hop.

The media spectacle has been stoked by a vocal anti-defamation position that reduces guido to a category of ethnic prejudice. While MTV may represent guido as uncool, anti-defamation diatribes disown guido as a vernacular Italian American culture. This is a position that ironically privileges the reality of media stereotypes.

Bibliography

Fikentscher, Kai. 2000. *'You Better Work!' Underground Dance Music in New York City*. Hanover and London: Wesleyan University.

Gladwell, Malcolm. 1997. "The Coolhunt," *The New Yorker*. March 17.

Lipsitz, Georg.e 1990. *Time Passages*. Minneapolis: University of Minnesota.

Maira, Sunaina. 2002. *Desis in the House*. Philadelphia: Temple University.

Maira, Sunaina and E. Soep. 2004. "United States of Adolescence?," *Young* 12.3: 245-69.

Thornton, Sarah. 1995. *Club Cultures*. Middleton: Wesleyan University Press.

Tricarico, Donald. 1984. *The Italians of Greenwich Village*. Staten Island: Center for Migration Studies.

_____ 2008. "Dressing Italian Americans for the Spectacle: What Difference Does Guido Perform?," *The Men's Fashion Reader*, edited by A. Reilly and S. Cosbey, New York: Fairchild. 265-78.

Willis, Paul 1990. *Common Cultures*. Boulder: Westview.

Keyword: Different. What Guidos Are, and Are Not
by Johnny DeCarlo

The guido/goomba/cugine is a very distinctive-looking, working-class east coast Italian-American. The whole lifestyle may seem shallow or strange to some, but "authentic" Italian-American life does not have to revolve around formal language, Renaissance art, or the opera. This is indeed a subculture that is very complex and needs exploration—not shunning and shame. There can be civil discussions about all these differences, but there should never be any mean-spirited debates on which one is right or wrong.

I'm a fan, follower, and researcher of all things Italian and Italian-American. Part of it stems, of course, from having Italian blood, and part of it is based directly on the fact that I personally feel that it is the most interesting and exciting culture of all. I love anything with roots from The Boot: books, TV shows, music, movies, fashion, cars, whatever else—especially culinary and religious traditions and practices. My mother speaks Italian fluently, I understand some and can identify meanings of words, and I am certainly fluent in linguine. I also incorporate words of different dialects into my speech patterns, which I call the goomba-Italiano (but I'll get into that later).

While I'm no expert, I certainly feel that I am not a faker or a poser like some out there who wrap themselves in the Italian flag to be cool, but can't even tell you the capital of Italy—or even worse—place a flag decal on their bumper backwards. I can say that I offer the unique perspective of having many guido Italian-American friends, Italian-Italian friends (direct immigrants), and everything in between. I grew up in the heart of it all and I've traveled to Italy as well.

The culture in Italy has its similarities and differences from the Italian-American culture here, so I think it's fair to say the Italian-American culture in the United States is a subculture in itself. Even if one is a direct immigrant and is trying to carry on the exact same lifestyle he or she had in Italy, it's still not going to be exactly the same—obviously because he or she is now in America. Then you have the children of those immigrants who have their own take on the Italian-American way, and then the children of those children. Within all that, there is yet another subculture with a controversial name: the guido subculture. What is this, and why is this controversial?

Well, what it's not is a subculture of the aforementioned posers and fakers who couldn't find Rome on the map. It's not just a group of ignorant kids who consume their lives with drinking, fighting, and having sex. The word itself is a describing word for this particular subculture, a light-hearted term of affection like goomba or cugine or paisan. It was never meant to be an offensive word like wop or guinea or greaseball, and it's unfortunate that many who are unaware of the true meanings associate the terms all together. And while a guido generally describes the single/under-30 generation, this isn't always the case as the guido is a constantly evolving creature. While carefree partying is often an aspect of the guido from the age of 17 until the mid-20s, this can be said of any group of individuals falling in that age range, regardless of nationality. If a guido is only consumed with partying 24/7 he has not yet evolved, but people in that age group should be able to enjoy themselves at a dance club or a bar from time to time, and shouldn't be labeled as unproductive members of society or as bad examples of Italian-Americans.

The guido/goomba/cugine is a very distinctive-looking, working-class east coast Italian-American (found in parts of New York/New Jersey/South Philly/Rhode Island, and a few other surrounding pockets). Steven Schirippa wrote three best-selling books on the subject. Yes, the guido is an outgoing, sometimes over-the-top type who may seem like a caricature, but that just stems from the east coast attitude in general. Yes, many stereotypes are played up like vanity or an affinity for Cadillacs and gold chains, but these particular stereotypes are not extremely harmful as many uptight (and out of touch) individuals claim—especially since they have validity and are not just done because of what's seen on TV. And whether one wants to acknowledge it or not, they do define this group of Italian Americans, so therefore, while we aren't talking about such high-culture things as opera music or Renaissance art, they are Italian-American things, and there are reasons for them. Having a particular car choice shared among guidos or a particular wardrobe (like a Fila tracksuit) is a shared social component identifying the group—and it's equally as valid as any other practice, belief, or style, even if it may seem unimportant to others.

When you take all of the children and grandchildren of Italian immigrants from all the different regions of The Boot and throw them together, you have your Little Italy neighborhoods on the east coast, and this guido subculture emerges. Things get translated and changed and carried onto the next generation, but the Italian root is still there, whether we are talking about a recipe or a word like *capicola* spoken as "ga-buh-gole" or calling pizza "ah-beetz" (the goomba-Italiano way). The whole lifestyle may seem shallow or strange to some—especially those who can't relate to it. The fact remains that "authentic" Italian-American life does not have to revolve around formal language, Renaissance art, or the opera—these things are just not for us all—but that does not make guidos less Italian or bad people. If they want to hang out at the corner pizza parlor instead of some black-tie restaurant, that does not make them classless. Just like someone doesn't have to be a rocket scientist and could be perfectly content as a plumber. This doesn't make him or her dumb. I know my heritage and I know the struggles. And I also know that even though a guido may not be "up to the standards" of some holier than thou folks, they do have pride.

Well-rounded people should not be treated or looked at poorly if they act a little silly from time to time, and to me, I find it disgusting that someone who shares Italian ancestry (these "activists") would look down on them because they may not share the exact same lifestyle. They just seem to look down on any Italian-American who is not in a certain social class and they want to classify this entire group (which is very large and very real) as fake, dumb, or bad people. That kind of behavior only points to their own insecurities. I thought only God is supposed to judge.

I'm only going to reference MTV's *Jersey Shore* once here. Reality shows are meant to play up the most dramatic and crazy moments—and the "cast members" are encouraged to ham it up for the camera. (Keep in mind that most who go on reality shows are aspiring entertainers.) No one really knows if their lives at home are consumed with what we see from a small sampling of a few months in a beach house. Within each of those housemate's worlds, they have their own lives and their own complexities just like every other person. I thought perhaps we could have seen some more of that on the show to balance things out. Maybe then there would be fewer haters, or it could have at least given more insight. There were a few episodes with genuine Italian-American family moments, but overall it's a fact that the shock TV stuff is what brings in the highest ratings. We'll have to wait for the new season to see whether or not redeeming qualities emerge or an evolution occurs for them. And if it does not, one should simply not tune into season two if shock TV is not your cup of tea. It's really nothing to demand boycotts over, as if we were watching them glorify murder. I say that because I am very tired of people equating the guido and the gangster as the same thing, as well. A guido or goomba may have parallels with a mobster, but nothing that pertains to the criminal aspects.

When *The Sopranos* was on, what I said to any Italian-American who had a problem with it was that yes, you can say they aren't great people based on the fact that they are Mafiosos, but many of their other aspects have direct parallels to a regular goomba from the neighborhood. And I'm speaking from the perspective of a lifelong Jersey paisan. The show was filmed right in my backyard. Their particular style of dress, food choices, and speech patterns—these are not made up words or bastardizations; the slang/dialect Italian is just part of it all.

I consider myself an evolved guido, just about to turn 30. That does not mean I am a "reformed" guido as if I have something to be ashamed of. I have a family, and my own catering business, and I have goals and aspirations. Do I still spike my hair up in the "Brooklyn blow-out" style and occasionally go to a dance club? Yes. But that does not consume my life and it never really did. But I know I am a good person and don't deserve any criticism if I do retain some of my guido practices or dress and speak a certain way. There needs to be more understanding of this whole thing so that automatic negative reactions aren't the norm.

Like Tony Manero, who really was the first guido showcased on film, it is indeed a subculture that is very complex and needs exploration—not shunning and shame. Manero, although flawed, had dreams and aspirations. We may not be perfect but if there are obvious redeeming qualities present, the guido is simply not a bad thing. Not many people recall the sequel to *Saturday Night Fever* which came out a few years later and showed Manero's evolution from dancing and hanging out in Brooklyn to making it on Broadway as a dancer. Why was that film not as successful as the original? No doubt because the partying aspects were not what the film focused on and that's simply too boring for mass audiences.

Years ago, immigrants felt the need to change their last name to assimilate. Should we tell every Italian-American to drop the vowel at the end of their names—from the highest scholar to the lowest guido? Because it can't go both ways here. We can't say it's OK for one Italian from one social class or one part of America to be proud of his background, yet guidos should be silenced because they are a little different. Look, nobody is perfect and nobody has the right to judge someone else's behavior—unless, of course, lines are crossed where laws are broken or where someone is being directly insulted.

I live my life and don't put down anyone—and you can't "insult" someone else by living your own life a certain way. We should all be fellow paisans—we are all from a different class or a different region in America—traced back to all the regions of Italy. And we all know there are vast differences there. Key word: different. Is there such a level of animosity between Italians in Venice and Italians in Sicily? As any casual observer of Italian studies can attest, yes, indeed this is how it was, but I would like to think that such feelings have evolved, too. If it is necessary, there can be civil discussions about all these differences, but there should never be any mean-spirited debates on which one is right or wrong, or any hating going on. Or you can do what I do, and just live your life one way and I'll happily live mine another. A person can be a staunch conservative and not believe in the gay lifestyle. Does that mean all conservatives *hate* gays? No. There are some who do that, and they are called extremists.

Thoughts from a Former Guidette—Turned Senator
By Diane Savino

I am a New York State Senator and certainly a strong defender of the Italian American community, but if you had asked me in 1981 to describe myself, I probably would have referred to myself as a guidette. It was never a negative thing; it was part of social identification for young people in a multiethnic city. Guido became acceptable or somehow desirable to those of us who were Italian Americans in the 1970s, when the movie Saturday Night Fever *changed the image for all of us. Then over the next five or six years, you started to see a lot of young Italian men emulating that look.*

So I hope that we can continue that discussion about who the real enemy is here; it's not the stereotypes that we've created for ourselves to make ourselves feel comfortable in our social identification. It is a fact that it has been exploited by people who have been exploiting our image in various ways, shapes, and forms for decades.

First, I want to thank the Institute for hosting this colloquium, and I want to thank all of you for coming. Yes, I am a New York state senator and certainly a strong defender of the Italian American community, but if you had asked me in 1981 to describe myself, I probably would have referred to myself as a guidette.

When the MTV show first came on and I saw the reaction to it by so many people, I was somewhat bemused by what I felt was an overreaction, which I think really ties back to the Italian American community's anger at mainstream media and the movie industry, and the way they have portrayed Italian Americans for decades. We have had numerous discussions about this in our community, whether it is the portrayal of all of us as gangsters, or the portrayal of all of us as buffoons, or all of the above.

But what I found most interesting was the reaction to the term guido as if it had not existed in Italian American culture for decades. Guido was never a pejorative when I was growing up, and in fact the idea of a guido, cugine, or cuginette, depending on where in New York City you lived and how you described yourself, dates even further back to probably the 1950s. At that time, when the term would have been "greaser," young Italian men wore leather jackets and had DA haircuts, and if they had curly hair they'd cut it really very short and they'd use Butch Wax to get it up. That's how my father dressed!

It was never a negative thing; it was part of social identification for young people in a multiethnic city. I think guido became acceptable or somehow desirable for those of us who were Italian Americans in the 1970s. And it is tied to three things in my opinion, and this is my own self-reflection from my own youth. One, of course, was adolescent anxiety. Another was music, and the influence of the media and music on young people. And, finally, there was a desire for those of us who were Italian American and who did not fit the standard of beauty at the time. If you think about it, in the 1970s the standard of beauty—for young girls, particularly—was the image we saw on *The Brady Bunch*, like Marcia: long straight blonde hair, very thin, very few curves. That was the standard of beauty.

The music of the time was rock 'n' roll, monster bands like Led Zeppelin, the Rolling Stones, and The Who. Along the way came the advent of this disco movement; and I remember when we were young, and I grew up in Astoria, there was this rivalry between people who were rock fans and disco fans—you couldn't be both! It was kind of silly and it was adolescent anxiety about how you identified yourself. And the one thing teenagers did not ever want was to be different from other teenagers. The uniform of the time for young people was ripped jeans and sneakers, and long hair, whether you were a boy or a girl. You wanted to look like the rock music icons that you saw; but many young Italian boys couldn't emulate that look, and neither could Italian girls. So we struggled with it; I always had long curly hair. That was not the standard of beauty then and probably isn't now, either. But I struggled for years to straighten my hair; I wanted to look like everyone else and I couldn't. I was overtly ethnic looking. I looked far more Italian than most Italian Americans with two Italian parents. I'm also the product of a mixed marriage, the Irish and the Italians. The outer boroughs of New York City were overwhelmingly populated by children who were either half-Irish or half-Italian, and how you identified yourself mattered; how you looked also helped determine that.

Then in 1977 along came a movie that changed the image for all of us, and that was *Saturday Night Fever*. I remember at the time I had a young friend, Angelo. Both of his parents were Italian, and he had incredibly curly hair that he grew out into an Afro. He learned how to play the drums; he wanted to be like John Bonham of Led Zeppelin. He would wear the uniform of the day: leather vest, no shirt, jeans, and torn sneakers, but he could never look like the other boys in the neighborhood. But he became a wicked drum player, and that was his dream. I remember standing on the corner of 35th Street in Astoria, like most teenagers did, and I looked down about two blocks away and saw this young man coming, in a white suit and shoes and a very short haircut. When he got closer to me I realized it was Angelo! He had changed his uniform; he had found something that he could identify with and was proud to look overtly Italian. I think at that moment in time I realized that the guido had been born. Then over the next five or six years, you started to see a lot of young Italian men emulating that look. As for young women, I could grow my hair out for the first time, let it be as curly and big as I wanted, and I didn't have to try to conform anymore. So for me, the development of the guido image was not a negative.

I went to St. John's University where we realized there were guidos in all parts of the city, from Staten Island to Queens to the Bronx. They were law school attendees; they were master's degree students. This was not a pejorative. It was simply a social identification, a way we could develop our own standard of beauty. We had our own uniform; and again, for young people the worse thing to be is unique. We like to think that young people dress a certain way because they are expressing their individuality. No, they're not; they don't want to express their individuality. They want to look like everybody else. So this was a way to look like everyone else who looked like us.

I'm somewhat bemused by the reaction to the guido and guidette phenomenon. It has always been a part of our culture in some way, shape, or form. It has never been a negative. What we should be angry about, and I think we really are on some level, is that MTV has chosen to take something and turn it into a pejorative. They deliberately sought out young Italian Americans who would be willing to go on TV and display their most aberrant behavior, and somehow, make the claim that that is symbolic of Italian Americans, or guidos/guidettes, or cugines/cuginettes, or however you want to call it. That is where our anger should be directed, not at the fact that this has been part of our culture. So I hope that we can continue that discussion about who the real enemy is here; it's not the stereotypes that we've created for ourselves to make ourselves feel comfortable in our social identification. It is the fact that it has been exploited by people who have been exploiting our image in various ways, shapes, and forms for decades.

Editors and Contributors

Editors

LETIZIA AIROS, author and journalist, is editor-in-chief of i-Italy (www.i-Italy.org), the first online multimedia magazine about Italy and Italian America, established in New York in 2008. She is co-founder and director of the Italian/American Digital Project, Inc. She has published *L'America da vicino, l'Italia da lontano: Italiani in America discutono l'11 settembre e le sue guerre* (Napoli, ESI, 2004).

OTTORINO CAPPELLI teaches political science at Università di Napoli "L'Orientale" in Italy, and is scholar-in-residence at the John D. Calandra Italian American Institute (Queens College, CUNY) where he directs the Oral History Archive. He is co-founder and vice president of the Italian/American Digital Project, Inc. and project manager of i-Italy (www.i-Italy.org). His most recent publication is "Re-interpreting Italian-American Politics: The Role of Ethnicity," in *The Status of Interpretation in Italian American Studies*, edited by Jerome Krase (New York: Stony Brook, 2011).

Contributors

NANCY C. CARNEVALE is associate professor of history at Montclair State University in New Jersey. She specializes in the history of immigration, race, and ethnicity in the U.S. with a focus on Italian immigration. Her most recent book is *A New Language, A New World: Italian Immigrants in the United States, 1890-1945* (2009).

DONNA CHIRICO is associate professor of psychology and chair of the Department of Behavioral Sciences at York College, CUNY.

FRED GARDAPHÉ is Distinguished Professor of Italian and Italian-American Studies at Queens College, CUNY. A prolific author in the field of Italian/American culture and literature, he is a member of the editorial board of i-Italy.

JOHNNY "MEATBALLS" DECARLO is part of an ensemble cast of the VH1 series, "My Big Friggin' Wedding," which is a reality show about planning his "ultimate Jersey Italian wedding" and the building of his "Johnny Meatballs Empire."

ALDO GRASSO, journalist and professor, teaches history of radio and television at Università Cattolica del Sacro Cuore in Milan, Italy. He is a media critic for the largest Italian daily newspaper, *Corriere della Sera*.

JEROME KRASE, a sociologist, is professor emeritus and Murray Koppelman Professor at Brooklyn College, CUNY. Author of several studies on ethnicity, race, and politics in urban America, he served as director of the Brooklyn College Center for Italian-American Studies and was a two-term president of the American Italian Historical Association. He is one of i-Italy's regular bloggers.

MARIA LAURINO is a writer and adjunct professor of creative writing at New York University. A former chief speechwriter to former New York City Mayor David Dinkins and a staff writer for the *Village Voice*, her books include *Were You Always an Italian?* (2001), a national best-selling memoir on ethnic identity, and more recently *Old World Daughter, New World Mother: An Education in Love and Freedom* (2009).

CHIARA MONTALTO is a playwright and performer. Her first solo play, *Emergency Used Candles*, was performed in New York City in 2010.

FRANCO MONTALTO teaches environmental engineering at Drexel University in Philadelphia.

GIANFRANCO NORELLI is a journalist and art director. His acclaimed documentary *Pane Amaro* [*Bitter Bread*], dedicated to the life and history of early Italian immigrants in the United States has recently been dubbed into English. He is a freelance consultant on special video projects for i-Italy.

LAURA RUBERTO is co-chair of the Arts and Cultural Studies Department at Berkeley City College in California, and author of *Gramsci, Migration, and the Representation of Women's Work in Italy and the U.S.* (2010). She has been blogging on i-Italy since its inception.

DIANE J. SAVINO is a Democratic Senator of the State of New York representing part of Brooklyn and Staten Island. She was a co-founder of the Working Families Party and has been President of the New York State Conference of Italian American Legislators.

JOSEPH SCIORRA, an ethno-folklorist specializing in Italian American studies, is associate director for academic and cultural programs at the John

D. Calandra Italian American Institute (Queens College, CUNY). Most recently he edited and contributed to *Italian Folk: Vernacular Culture in Italian-American Lives* (2010). He regularly blogs on i-Italy as Joey Skee.

ANTHONY JULIAN TAMBURRI is dean of the John D. Calandra Italian American Institute (Queens College, CUNY) and professor of Italian and Italian/American Studies. A semiotician by training, he has written extensively on Italian and Italian/American literature and films. He is president of the Italian American Digital Project, Inc. and member of the editorial board of i-Italy. His latest book is *Reviewing Italian Americana: Generalities and Specificities on Cinema* (2011).

DONALD TRICARICO, professor of sociology in the Department of Social Sciences, Queensborough, CUNY, specializes in youth urban subcultures and racial and ethnic relations. He is a recognized authority in the field of Italian/American youth styles and the guido subculture in particular.

ROBERT VISCUSI, writer and professor, is the director of the Ethyle R. Wolfe Institute for the Humanities at Brooklyn College, CUNY, as well as president of the Italian American Writers Association. Author among other works, his novel *Astoria* (1995) won the American Book Award in 1996. He is a member of the editorial board of i-Italy.

Index of Names

Abdel-Hardy, Dalia, 58
Alba, Richard, 58
Alighieri, Dante, 27, 33
Angelina (from *Jersey Shore*), 56, 60
Airos, Letizia, 9, 21, 89, 101, 125
Ardizzone, Tony, 71

Bacarella, Michael, 71
Barth, Fredrik, 41, 43
Beiner, Ronald, 21
Berlusconi, Silvio, 33, 34, 90, 91, 96
Bonham, John, 123
Bonsaver, Guido, 27
Bosworth, R, J. B., 26, 29
Brando, Marlon, 79, 80
Brooks, Caryn, 44

Calandra John D., 54
Cannistraro, Philip, 18, 28, 30, 42, 43,
Cappelli, Ottorino, 13, 19, 75, 79, 83, 86, 101, 125
Carnevale, Nancy, 83, 125
Cavaricci, Z., 63, 64
Cavour, Camillo Benso, 26
Chase, David, 71
Choate, Mark I., 28
Chirico, Donna M., 79, 125
Ciabattari, Mark, 71
Cohen, Nick, 76
Cohen, Patricia, 17
Columbus, Christopher, 33, 42, 83, 84
Connell, William J., 19
Coppola, Francis Ford, 71, 93
Cosby, Bill 71, 104
Covello, Leonard, 85

D'Azeglio, Massimo, 26
Dahl, Robert, 24
DeCarlo, Johnny, 14, 17, 40, 59, 101, 115, 126
Dean, James, 79, 80
De Niro, Robert, 31
DeStefano, George, 19
deVries, Rachel Guido, 71
DiMaggio, Joe, 31
DiMino, Andrè, 19, 57
Dinkins, David, 52
DuBois, W.E.B., 71

Eco, Umberto, 13, 20
Ermelino, Louise, 71

Farella, Chickie, 71
Farini, Luigi Carlo, 26
Fikentscher, Kai, 108, 114
Fini, Gianfranco, 34, 89
Frida Kahlo, 63

Galilei, Galileo, 58
Gardaphè, Fred, 19, 20, 40, 44, 51, 54, 69, 101, 125
Gerratana, Valentino, 26
Gillan, Maria Mazziotti, 71
Gladwell, Malcolm, 106, 114
Gotti, John, 112 (as person), 113 (in show title)
Gramsci, Antonio, (5), 26, 67, 68 (126)
Grasso, Aldo, 11, 21, 32, 89, 125
Graziano, Manlio, 25
Guglielmo, Jennifer, 29
Guglielmo, Thomas A., 29

Hays, William H., 69

Hardy, Ed, 113
Harney, Robert F., 42, 43
Hebdige, Dick, 65
Hendin, Josephine Gattuso, 71
Hill, Henry, 53
Hopper, Dennis, 67
Hewitt, Roger, 33

Ingrasciotta, Frank, 71

JWoww (from *Jersey Shore*), 56, 60

Krase, Jerome, 33, 50, 71, 125, 126
Knapp, Whitman (Knapp Commission), 53

Laurino, Maria, 20, 21, 75, 126
LaGuardia, Fiorello, 69
Lee, Spike, 71
Lentricchia, Frank, 71
Lipsitz, George, 107, 108, 114

Madonna (Louise Ciccone), 103
Maira, Sunaina, 107, 114
Manzi, Alberto, 92
Martin, Dick, 31
McLuhan, Marshall, 9
Montalto, Chiara, 63, 126
Montanto, Franco, 63, 126
Musolino, Michela, 71
Mussolini, Benito, 18, 26, 27, 28, 29, 30, 43

Norelli, Gianfranco, 71, 86, 126

Obama, Barack Hussein, 51

Pacino, Al, 31
Pamuk, Ohran, 20, 78
Pasquino, 68

Pauly D (from *Jersey Shore*), 56, 57, 60
Petraccone, Claudia, 26
Plath, Sylvia, 63
Postiglione, Corey, 71
Prezzolini, Giuseppe, 28
Poussaint, Alvin, 104

Rimanelli, Giose, 71
Ronnie (from *Jersey Shore*), 56
Ruberto, Laura, 67, 126

Salvemini, Gaetano, 28,
Salerno, Salvatore, 29
Sammi "Sweetheart" (from *Jersey Shore*), 56, 60
Santucci, Antonio A., 26
Savino, Diane, 17, 121, 126
Savoca, Nancy, 71
Schempp, William, 101
Sciorra, Joseph, 39, 65, 101, 126
Scorsese, Martin, 31, 71
Sinatra, Frank, 31, 79, 80
Snooki (from *Jersey Shore*), 56, 58, 60, 81
Soep, Elisabeth, 107, 114
Sorrentino, Frank M., 33

Tamburri, Anthony Julian, 13, 101, 127
The Situation (Mike Sorrentino; from *Jersey Shore*), 55, 56, 60, 61, 62, 72
Thornton, Sarah, 108, 114
Timpanelli, Gioia, 71
Travolta, John, 39, 76, 77, 119
Tresca, Carlo, 18
Tricarico, Donald, 14, 15, 16, 17, 40, 41, 42, 43, 45, 46, 47, 51,

54, 59, 101, 106, 107, 110, 114, 127

Valerio, Anthony, 71
Vinny (from *Jersey Shore*), 56, 61
Viscusi, Robert, 30, 55, 127

Williams, Wendy, 58
Willis, Paul, 109, 114

Zandy, Janet, 71

VIA FOLIOS

A refereed book series dedicated to Italian Studies and the culture of Italian Americans in North America and other areas of the Italian diaspora.

FRED GARDAPHÉ
Moustache Pete Is Dead
Vol. 67, Oral Literature, $12.00

PAOLO RUFFILLI
Dark Room • Camera oscura
Vol. 66, Poetry, $11.00

HELEN BAROLINI
Crossing the Alps
Vol. 65, Novel, $15.00

COSMO FERRARO, ED.D.
Profiles of Italian Americans
Vol. 64, Essay, $16.00

GIL FAGIANI
Chianti in Connecticut
Vol. 63, Poetry, $10.00

PIERO BASSETTI
Italic Lessons: An On-going Dialog
Vol. 62, Essay, $10.00

GRACE CAVALIERI & SABINE PESCARELLI, EDS.
The Poet's Cookbook
Vol. 61, Poetry & Recipes, $12.00

EMANUEL DI PASQUALE
Siciliana
Vol. 60, Poetry, $8.00

NATALIA COSTA-ZALESSOW, ED.
Francesca Turini Bufalini:
Autobiographical Poems
Vol. 59, Poetry, $20.00

RICHARD VETERE
Baroque
Vol. 58, Fiction, $18.00

LEWIS TURCO
La Famiglia/The Family
Vol. 57, Memoir, $15.00

NICK JAMES MILETI
The Unscrupulous
Vol. 56, Art Criticism, $20.00

PIERO BASSETTI
Italici
Vol. 55, Essay, $8.00

GIOSE RIMANELLI
The Three-Legged One
Vol. 54, Fiction, $15.00

CHARLES KLOPP
Bele Antiche Stòrie
Vol. 53, Criticism, $25.00

JOSEPH RICAPITO
Second Wave
Vol. 52, Poetry, $12.00

GARY MORMINO
Italians in Florida
Vol. 51, History, $15.00

GIANFRANCO ANGELUCCI
Federico F.
Vol. 50, Fiction, $16.00

ANTHONY VALERIO
The Little Sailor
Vol. 49, Memoir, $9.00

ROSS TALARICO
The Reptilian Interludes
Vol. 48, Poetry, $15.00

RACHEL GUIDO DEVRIES
Teeny Tiny Tino
Vol. 47, Children's Lit., $6.00

EMANUEL DIPASQUALE
Writing Anew
Vol. 46, Poetry, $15.00

MARIA FAMÀ
Looking for Cover
Vol. 45, Poetry, $15.00 / CD, $6.00

ANTHONY VALERIO
Tony Cade Bambara's One Sicilian Night
Vol. 44, Memoir, $10.00

EMANUEL CARNEVALI
DENNIS BARONE, ED. & AFTERWORD
Furnished Rooms
Vol. 43, Poetry, $14.00

BRENT ADKINS, ET.AL
Shifting Borders
Vol. 42, Cultural Criticism, $18.00

Published by BORDIGHERA, INC., an independently owned not-for-profit scholarly organization that has no legal affiliation to the University of Central Florida or the John D. Calandra Italian American Institute, Queens College, City University of New York.

GEORGE GUIDA
Low Italian
Vol. 41, Poetry, $11.00

GARDAPHÉ, GIORDANO, AND TAMBURRI
Introducing Italian Americana:
Generalities on Literature and Film
Vol. 40, Criticism $10.00

DANIELA GIOSEFFI
Blood Autumn/Autunno di sangue
Vol. 39, Poetry, $15.00/$25.00

FRED MISURELLA
Lies to Live by
Vol. 38, Stories, $15.00

STEVEN BELLUSCIO
Constructing a Bibliography
Vol. 37, Italian Americana, $15.00

ANTHONY JULIAN TAMBURRI, ED.
Italian Cultural Studies 2002
Vol. 36, Essays, $18.00

BEA TUSIANI
con amore
Vol. 35, Memoir, $19.00

FLAVIA BRIZIO-SKOV, ED.
Reconstructing Societies in the
Aftermath of War
Vol. 34, History/Cultural Studies,
$30.00

ANTHONY JULIAN TAMBURRI et al
Italian Cultural Studies 2001
Vol. 33, Essays, $18.00

ELIZABETH GIOVANNAMESSINA,
ED.
In Our Own Voices
Vol. 32, Ital. Amer. Studies, $25.00

STANISLAO G. PUGLIESE
Desperate Inscriptions
Vol. 31, History, $12.00

HOSTERT & TAMBURRI, EDS.
Screening Ethnicity
Vol. 30, Ital. Amer. Culture, $25.00

G. PARATI & B. LAWTON, EDS.
Italian Cultural Studies
Vol. 29, Essays, $18.00

HELEN BAROLINI
More Italian Hours & Other Stories
Vol. 28, Fiction, $16.00

FRANCO NASI, ed.
Intorno alla Via Emilia
Vol. 27, Culture, $16.00

ARTHUR L. CLEMENTS
The Book of Madness and Love
Vol. 26, Poetry, $10.00

JOHN CASEY, ET AL.
Imagining Humanity
Vol. 25, Interdisciplinary Studies,
$18.00

ROBERT LIMA
Sardinia • Sardegna
Vol. 24, Poetry, $10.00

DANIELA GIOSEFFI
Going On
Vol. 23, Poetry, $10.00

ROSS TALARICO
The Journey Home
Vol. 22, Poetry, $12.00

EMANUEL DIPASQUALE
The Silver Lake Love Poems
Vol. 21, Poetry, $7.00

JOSEPH TUSIANI
Ethnicity
Vol. 20, Selected Poetry, $12.00

JENNIFER LAGIER
Second Class Citizen
Vol. 19, Poetry, $8.00

FELIX STEFANILE
The Country of Absence
Vol. 18, Poetry, $9.00

PHILIP CANNISTRARO
Blackshirts
Vol. 17, History, $12.00

LUIGI RUSTICHELLI, ED.
Seminario sul racconto
Vol. 16, Narrativa, $10.00

LEWIS TURCO
Shaking the Family Tree
Vol. 15, Poetry, $9.00

LUIGI RUSTICHELLI, ED.
Seminario sulla drammaturgia
Vol. 14, Theater/Essays, $10.00

FRED L. GARDAPHÈ
Moustache Pete is Dead!
Vol. 13, Oral literature, $10.00

JONE GAILLARD CORSI
Il libretto d'autore, 1860–1930
Vol. 12, Criticism, $17.00

HELEN BAROLINI
Chiaroscuro: Essays of Identity
Vol. 11, Essays, $15.00

T. PICARAZZI & W. FEINSTEIN, EDS.
An African Harlequin in Milan
Vol. 10, Theater/Essays, $15.00

JOSEPH RICAPITO
Florentine Streets and Other Poems
Vol. 9, Poetry, $9.00

FRED MISURELLA
Short Time
Vol. 8, Novella, $7.00

NED CONDINI
Quartettsatz
Vol. 7, Poetry, $7.00

A. J. TAMBURRI, ED. & M. J. BONA,
INTROD.
*Fuori: Essays by Italian/American
Lesbians and Gays*
Vol. 6, Essays, $10.00

ANTONIO GRAMSCI
P. VERDICCHIO, TRANS. & INTROD.
The Southern Question
Vol. 5, Social Criticism, $5.00

DANIELA GIOSEFFI
Word Wounds and Water Flowers
Vol. 4, Poetry, $8.00

WILEY FEINSTEIN
*Humility's Deceit: Calvino Reading
Ariosto Reading Calvino*
Vol. 3, Criticism, $10.00

PAOLO A. GIORDANO, ED.
*Joseph Tusiani:
Poet, Translator, Humanist*
Vol. 2, Criticism, $25.00

ROBERT VISCUSI
*Oration Upon the Most Recent Death
of Christopher Columbus*
Vol. 1, Poetry, $3.00

CPSIA information can be obtained at www.ICGtesting.com
Printed in the USA
BVOW031203071011

272995BV00001B/6/P